7/22/20
$25.00

I'M STILL HERE

I'M STILL HERE

BLACK DIGNITY IN A WORLD MADE FOR WHITENESS

AUSTIN CHANNING BROWN

CONVERGENT

New York

Copyright © 2018 by Austin Channing Brown

All rights reserved.
Published in the United States by Convergent Books, an imprint of the Crown Publishing Group, a division of
Penguin Random House LLC, New York.
convergentbooks.com

CONVERGENT BOOKS is a registered trademark and its C colophon is a trademark of Penguin Random House LLC.

The chapter "Why I Love Being a Black Girl" was originally published in a different form at austinchanningbrown.com, in 2015.

Library of Congress Cataloging-in-Publication Data is available.

ISBN 978-1-5247-6085-4
Ebook ISBN 978-1-5247-6086-1

Printed in the United States of America

Jacket design by Na Kim

20 19 18 17

I dedicate this book to

G. Jacqueline Holley, my grandmother,

who is the personification of

Black dignity and love.

CONTENTS

Contents

I'M STILL HERE

1

White People Are Exhausting

White people can be exhausting. Particularly exhausting are white people who don't know they are white, and those who need to be white. But of all the white people I've met—and I've met a lot of them in more than three decades of living, studying, and working in places where I'm often the only Black woman in sight—the first I found exhausting were those who expected *me* to be white.

To be fair, my parents did set them up for failure. In this society where we believe a name tells us everything we need to know about someone's race, gender, income, and personality, my parents decided to outwit everyone by giving their daughter a white man's name. When I was growing up, they explained that my grandmother's maiden name was

Austin, and since her only brother didn't have children, they wanted to make me the last Austin of our family line.

Sounds beautiful, right? Well, it is. It just happens to be half the story.

How did I discover the other half? Through my exhaustion with a white person. We were in my favorite place—our local library, built in a square with an outdoor garden at the center. At seven years old, with books piled high in my arms, I often had to be reminded how many I had already checked out when it came time for our next visit. I am certain my family singlehandedly kept our library funded. We checked out so many books at a time, we would find them under the car seat, between the cushions of our couch, or hiding under the mail on the table.

On this sunny Saturday afternoon, as I stepped up to the front desk to check out my books, I remember the librarian taking my library card and scanning the back as usual. I braced myself, expecting her to announce the fine I owed for the week.

Instead, she raised one eyebrow as the other furrowed and asked, "Is this your card?"

Wondering for a split second if I'd mixed up my card with my mother's, I nodded my head yes, but hesitantly. "Are you sure?" she said. "This card says Austin."

I nodded more emphatically and smiled. "Yes, that's my card." Perhaps she was surprised a first-grader could rack up such a fine. But when I peered over the counter, I saw that she still hadn't opened the book covers to stamp the day when I should bring them back (emphasis on *should*). I waited.

"Are you sure this is your card?" she asked again, this time drawing out *sure* and *your* as if they had more than one syllable. I tilted my head in exasperation, rolling my eyes toward the popcorn ceiling. Did she not see all the recent books on my account? Surely this woman didn't think I didn't know my own name.

Then it dawned on me. She wasn't questioning my literacy. She was another in an already long line of people who couldn't believe my name belonged to me. With a sigh too deep for my young years, I replied, "Yes, my name is Austin, and that is my library card." She stammered something about my name being unusual as her eyebrows met. I didn't respond. I just waited for her to hand my books back to me.

My check-outs in hand, I marched over to my mother, who was standing in the VHS section with my little brother. I demanded that she tell me why she named me Austin.

By then, I had gotten used to white people

expecting me to be male. It happened every first day of school, at roll call. The boys and girls automatically gravitated to opposite sides of the room, and when my name was called, I had to do jumping jacks to get the teacher's attention away from the "boys' section." So how did I know this wasn't more of the same? The woman's suspicion. Because, after I answered her question about my little library card, I still was not believed. I couldn't have explained it at the time, but I knew this was about more than me not being a boy.

"Why did you give me this name?" I demanded, letting my books fall loudly on the table next to us. My mother, probably wondering how she'd managed to raise a little Judy Blume character of her own, started retelling the story of my grandmother and the Austin family. But I cut her off. "Momma, I know *how* you came up with my name, but why did you choose it?"

She walked me over to a set of scratchy green armchairs and started talking in a slow, soothing voice. "Austin, your father and I had a really hard time coming up with a name that we both liked. One of us thought to use your grandmother's maiden name—her last name before she married your grandfather." I already knew this part of the story. I swung my legs impatiently, waiting for her to tell me more.

"As we said it aloud, we loved it," she continued. "We knew that anyone who saw it before meeting you would assume you are a white man. One day you will have to apply for jobs. We just wanted to make sure you could make it to the interview."

My mother watched my face, waiting for a reaction. My brain scrolled through all the times a stranger had said my name but wasn't talking to me. In every instance, the intended target had been not only a boy but a white boy. I didn't quite understand my mother's point about job applications—to that point, the only application I had filled out was probably for the library card in my hand. But one thing became clear. People's reaction to my name wasn't just about my gender. It was also about my brown skin. My legs stilled. That's why the librarian hadn't believed me. She didn't know a name like Austin could be stretched wide enough to cloak a little Black girl.

As I grew older, my parents' plan worked—almost too well. To this day, I receive emails addressed to "Mr. Austin Brown" and voice mails asking if Mr. Brown can please return their call. When I am being introduced to new people, there is often an attempt to feminize my name ("You mean Autumn?") or to assign my name to my husband. And though I usually note that I am a Black woman in my cover letters, I nonetheless surprise hiring committees when I show up to the interview in all my melanin glory.

Heading into the meeting, I'm dressed up and nervous. Typically I have made it beyond the essay-writing stage, the personality test, or the phone interview with HR. This in-person group interview is usually the final step. I sit in the lobby waiting for someone to collect me. An assistant comes around the corner and looks at me, wondering if I could possibly be the next candidate. A little tentative in case a grave mistake has been made, he asks, "Are you Austin?"

I reply with an enthusiastic yes, pretending I didn't notice the look of panic that they'd accidentally invited a Black girl to the interview. The tension eases for him as it grips the muscle under my right shoulder blade. I silently take a couple deep breaths as I follow him to the conference room. "Everyone, this is Austin . . ."

Every pair of eyes looks at me in surprise. They look at the person next to them. They blink. Then they look down at my résumé. Every. Single. Time.

The person who walked me into the room is still talking, but no one is listening. They are all combing my résumé looking for clues. Should they have known? Am I now more impressive or less impressive? What does this mean for the position? For the partners? For the team? They weren't prepared for this. They were expecting a white man.

It would be comical if it wasn't so damn disappointing.

Thanks to the progressive circles I usually travel in, most people want to be excited by the "mistake" and ignore all the thoughts, the questions, the change that happened when my body stood before them. But that moment cannot be ignored. The thoughts and questions may dissipate from the interview but never from the mind, the heart. For this becomes the unspoken question for my entire time with an organization: *Are we sure she will be a good fit?* Or, said another way, *Since we didn't vet her knowing she is a Black woman, are we sure she'll fit in with our [white] culture? Or should we have hired the white person who came next?*

I cannot speak for every Black woman navigating white culture, but this is how being hired usually unfolds for me:

First, I am given a promise, usually from a

supervisor, co-worker, or member of the hiring committee, that she is a safe person for me to talk to if anything racist happens. To make the promise of safety feel genuine, she admits that the organization isn't perfect and assures me that I can share if there is ever an inappropriate comment, a wrong word. That way, the problem can be addressed. Second, I am given a brief account of the organization's imperfections, a series of stories involving elusive people who no longer belong to the organization. The stories usually concern examples of "missteps"—the time a white person "misspoke" in a board meeting or when a racist email was intercepted by leadership—but they end on a note of hope, expressing how the organization reacted. *We invited* [insert name of famous Black person] *to speak at our annual lunch. We launched an eight-week discussion group on* [book by Black author].

But within my first few weeks of working there, the organization's stereotypes, biases, or prejudices begin to emerge. Comments about my hair. Accolades for being "surprisingly articulate" or "particularly entertaining." Requests to "be more Black" in my speech. Questions about single moms, the hood, "black-on-black crime," and other hot topics I am supposed to know all about because I'm Black.

So I bring up the incidents with my safe person—the one who said she wants to know about these encounters—but the response is some version of "Perhaps you misunderstood" or "I'm sure he didn't mean it like that." Oftentimes the responsibility to extend compassion falls on me. "You really ought to go back to talk to him. Perhaps if you were more patient, you could see his heart." So I move on. Rather than dwell on individuals, I speak about the system. About white boardrooms and white leadership teams. About white culture and the organization's habit of hiring people who perpetuate that culture rather than diversify it. But the white consensus doesn't want me to point out these things. I was only supposed to name the "bad apples," so now whiteness has a few names for me. *Divisive. Negative. Toxic.*

I feel disappointed. I had hoped that this organization, this group of people, might be different from the last one—that they would understand what it means to embody an organization's diversity in more than numbers. But instead of giving up, I take a step back. I return to pointing out the "bad apples," hoping that my doing so will lead others to see the systemic. I talk about the woman who touched my hair without permission, and the man who called me "colored" in the hallway. I talk about how when I walk into our church, people still ask me if I am looking for the food pantry. How they greet me as a newcomer every Sunday, even though I have not changed my seat in two years.

I am not interested in getting anyone in trouble; I am trying to clarify what it's like to exist in a Black body in an organization that doesn't understand it is not only Christian but also white. But instead of offering empathy and action, whiteness finds new names for me and offers ominous advice. I am too sensitive, and should be careful with what I report. I am too angry, and should watch my tone when I talk about my experiences. I am too inflexible, and should learn to offer more grace to people who are really trying.

It's exhausting.

White people who expect me to be white have not yet realized that their cultural way of being is not in fact the result of goodness, rightness, or God's blessing. Pushing back, resisting the lie, is hella work.

It's work to be the only person of color in an organization, bearing the weight of all your white co-workers' questions about Blackness.

It's work to always be hypervisible because of

your skin—easily identified as being present or absent—but for your needs to be completely invisible to those around you.

It's work to do the emotional labor of pointing out problematic racist thinking, policies, actions, and statements while desperately trying to avoid bitterness and cynicism.

It's work to stay open to an organization to learn new skills without drinking in the cultural expectations of body size, personality, interests, and talents most valued according to whiteness.

Quite frankly, the work isn't just tedious. It can be dangerous for Black women to attempt to carve out space for themselves—their perspective, their gifts, their skills, their education, their experiences—in places that haven't examined the prevailing assumption of white culture. The danger of letting whiteness walk off with our joy, our peace, our sense of dignity and self-love, is ever present. But it doesn't have to be this way. Togetherness across racial lines doesn't have to mean the uplifting of whiteness and harming of Blackness. And even though the Church I love has been the oppressor as often as it has been the champion of the oppressed, I can't let go of my belief in Church—in a universal body of belonging, in a community that reaches toward love in a world so often filled with hate. I continue to be drawn toward the collective participation of seeking good, even when that means critiquing the institution I love for its commitment to whiteness.

This book is my story about growing up in a Black girl's body. There is nothing profound about where my story takes place. I didn't grow up in another country, in the Deep South or the hood. I grew up around white people in a family-friendly middle-class neighborhood. There was neither devastating poverty nor incredible wealth, and the demographics of my neighborhood and schools often mimicked America as a whole—mostly white, but never exclusively so.

I also grew up in the late eighties and early nineties, the height of America's supposed commitment to racial color blindness. At my Christian elementary school, we sang, "Jesus loves the little children . . . red and yellow, black and white, all are precious in his sight." In alignment with this song, white people often professed, "I don't even see color," reassuring me that I would be safe from racism with them. And yet, I learned pretty early in life that while Jesus may be cool with racial diversity, America is not. The ideology that whiteness is supreme, better, best, permeates the air we breathe—in our schools, in our offices, and in our country's common life. White supremacy is a tradition that must be named and a religion that must be renounced. When this work has not been done, those who live in whiteness become oppressive, whether intentional or not.

I learned about whiteness up close. In its classrooms and hallways, in its offices and sanctuaries. At the same time, I was also learning about Blackness, about myself, and about my faith. My story is not about condemning white people but about rejecting the assumption—sometimes spoken, sometimes not—that white is right: closer to God, holy, chosen, the epitome of being. My story is about choosing to love my Black femaleness, even when it shocks folks who expected someone quite different. It's about standing before roomfuls of Christians and challenging them to see Blackness without the baggage of racist bias. It's about surviving in a world not made for me—where my parents tried to arm me with the cultural cash of a white, male name.

I offer this story in hopes that we will embody a community eager to name whiteness, celebrate Blackness, and, in a world still governed by systems of racial oppression, begin to see that there's another way.

2

Playing Spades

I had to learn what it really means to love Blackness. I hate to admit it, but it's true.

My parents' home was a Black family's home. Framed posters of Alvin Ailey dancers were suspended on the walls and the words of Alice Walker, Toni Morrison, Langston Hughes, and other Black authors occupied every inch of space on maple-colored bookshelves. On Saturday mornings, Luther Vandross crooned from our record player as we completed our chores. Afterward, as a reward, Mom and Dad twirled us around the family room, practicing the Cleveland hand dance. At the dinner table they stuffed us with stories of Black achievement and wondered aloud about the color barriers we would break when we got older . . . But however hard my parents worked to instill in me pride in being Black, their arms weren't long enough to reach beyond the walls of our family.

My elementary school was predominately white. From pre-K all the way through eighth grade, I was always just one of a handful of Black students in my classes—but because I had attended that school longer than most of the teachers had worked there, I walked the hallways like I owned the place. Not that I didn't notice differences between myself and the white girls in my classroom. I wondered why their ponytails swung side to side but mine bounced up and down. I wondered why all the characters in my school's library books seemed obsessed with campfires and playing the guitar on a beach, and I also noticed that none of my teachers looked like me.

But rather than my race being the elephant in the room, it seemed instead to be my secret knowledge. I knew all about the world of my white teachers and peers, but they didn't seem to know a thing about mine. Teachers never referenced television shows my family wouldn't miss—*A Different World*; *Sister, Sister*; or *Moesha*. Our school praised the music of Amy Grant, DC Talk, and Michael W. Smith, but never mentioned gospel artists like Babbie Mason, Helen Baylor, Fred Hammond, and

Kirk Franklin. Conversations that filled the air in my household never would've happened with my teachers.

For example, I remember one Christmas weekend when I was eleven or twelve, my family gathered in my grandmother's home in Cleveland. My grandparents, aunts, uncles, and cousins sat around two tables—one for the adults, one for the kids— separated by a short open bookshelf filled with vintage bells my grandmother had collected over decades. From my folding chair at the kids' table, I peered through the gaps in the shelves, trying to follow the adults' conversation as my mom went toe-to-toe with the men sitting across from her.

"I'm just not sure integration has actually helped Black Americans," she said. Her hands danced in front of her as she continued the impassioned monologue, her afro nodding in agreement.

"Well, what was the alternative, Karen?" one of my uncles retorted. "Remaining in segregation?"

Her eyes flashed. She knew she had them. "Of course not. I'm just saying that *segregation* didn't have to be followed with *integration*. Surely relegating us to the back of the bus could have stopped without us having to give up all the businesses that died because we started going to white folks. Think about all that we lost—the doctors' and dentists' offices, the grocery store owners and auto mechanics. I mean, could we have kept a great number of Black teachers if we had demanded equal funding for our schools rather than busing ourselves to theirs?"

The debate continued, deep voices rising and falling, conceding and breaking away. Conversations like this were normal with this crew, but my white school was different. There, we weren't supposed to question history. We were expected to learn the names of Rosa Parks and Martin Luther King Jr., thank God that we could all share an integrated classroom now, and move on to another lesson with hearts of gratitude.

But we weren't always grateful to be with the white kids.

I think I was in the fourth grade when it first happened. My classmates and I were lining up to leave for gym class or perhaps art or music class. I was standing toward the back of the line when a short white boy, Zach, stood in front of me and mumbled something about monkeys and bananas, looking at no one in particular.

"What?" I responded, genuinely confused. I glanced at the bulletin boards around the room, searching for a good reason he would be talking about monkeys.

Zach turned all the way around to stare up into my eyes. "Nigger," he said.

Everything stopped. The twelve kids in front of him disappeared as my eyes narrowed. My stomach lurched. I had always thought of myself as a nice kid, the kind who gets along with her classmates. But in this moment I had a feeling I was about to surprise myself. I don't remember exactly what I retorted, but I do know that I wasn't silent, and I know it was mean, because Zach never tried that shit again.

My parents never sat me down to tell me what I should do if a white person called me a nigger, and I was too young to know the history of that word at the time. But there was one thing I knew for sure. My anger was justified. And though I never got "The Talk" about the n–word, my parents did give me plenty of other examples about the ways a white person might try me.

Following my dad through the toy section of the party store, I picked up a little trinket that caught my attention. "Don't even think about it," he said, shooting me down before I could debate whether or not to ask him to buy it. I sighed, put the trinket back, and stuffed my hands in the pockets of my overalls, willing myself not to be tempted again.

My father glanced back at me, but when he noticed my little fists bulging from my pockets, he stopped in the middle of the aisle and turned all the way around. "Don't do that," he said sternly.

Do what? I wondered to myself. I had long ago learned to tame my smart mouth with my dad. Was he now reading my mind?

"Don't ever do that," he repeated more softly this time, bending his six-foot-two frame toward me to let me know I wasn't in trouble. But I was still confused. What had I done wrong?

"Even if you put it back on the shelf, Austin, you can't touch store products and then put your hands in your pockets," he explained as his large hands gently removed mine from their denim hiding place. "Someone might notice and assume you are trying to steal."

I nodded. It took some time, but eventually I trained myself not to touch my pockets—and nowadays, my purse—when walking through store aisles.

Then there was the moment when my mom took me to the mall to buy my first CD. I spent far longer than I should have combing through the thin boxes, deciding between new releases from Boyz II Men, Aaliyah, Mariah Carey, Tevin Campbell, and SWV. I chose Mariah Carey's *Music Box,* took it to the front of the line, and paid for it with the little cash I had. On our way out of the store, I tore into the plastic, opening the CD liner, where artists kept photos and lyrics.

"Whoa, Daughter," my mother warned. I looked at her quizzically, wondering if I had shown too much excitement. Even the cashier paused for a moment, surprised by her sudden forcefulness.

"You never open an item in the store, and always have the receipt in your hand if you do," my mother said. "You always want to be able to show someone you paid for your things." It's funny how in these little life lessons, I always knew that "someone" was white people.

My parents made sure I knew that at any moment when I wasn't paying attention, when I was just being a person, everything could be interrupted. *Be careful with white people* was the message I received loud and clear. But strangely enough, it was being around Black kids that turned out to be harder for me . . . at first.

It happened when I was ten. My parents got divorced, and my little brother and I started spending summers in Cleveland with my mother. Cleveland was only two hours away from my home in Toledo, but the move from a mostly white setting into one that was all Black made our new neighborhood feel like a different planet. It was the first time I had ever walked into a public sphere where the majority of people looked like me. The culture shock was glorious and terrifying.

At first, I didn't understand the culture I had landed in. I wasn't prepared for the loudness, the playfulness. I didn't know about dance competitions and talent shows, and I didn't know there were more line dances than the Electric Slide. (The Tootsie Roll was a complete takeover that summer.) Kids and adults here cursed on a regular basis. There were no games reciting the books of the Bible at the day camp our mother enrolled us in; I had to learn to play Spades in this joint.

It was hard to keep up. When the popular song "Weak" by SWV came on the radio, our entire bus started singing it on the way to the community pool. I had never heard the song before, so I attempted to lip-synch the whole thing, praying that the girls around me would continue singing with their eyes closed instead of noticing me. I listened to the Black radio station all summer after that, trying to learn the popular songs. But no matter how hard I worked to pretend this new world made sense to me, there was so much I didn't know. I had no idea who Bobby Brown was, or why Whitney Houston shouldn't marry him. And I didn't know why the girls at day camp dared me to say "Candyman" five times in the bathroom mirror. On the fifth time, they all screamed, so I screamed, too. I had no idea what I was supposed to be afraid of. The only thing I feared was being discovered.

Here in Cleveland, other Black children called me Oreo and were curious about why I "talked white." I didn't know what to say the first time someone told me that. *Well, I only live here during the summers . . . I actually live in Toledo with my dad and go to a school that looks nothing like this neighborhood . . . All my teachers have been white and most of my classmates, too . . . So I guess that's why I talk white?* Kids didn't have time for all that, and I wasn't mature enough to question the question. But still, it hurt. I was working so hard to hide the culture of whiteness, only to discover that it was dripping from my body, pouring from my throat. All I wanted was to fit in, but everyone knew I was pretending.

It was draining—to the point where I sometimes feigned being sick. I would find a table as far from everyone as I could and put my head down. When a counselor came to check on me, I would squint as if the light was hurting my eyes and explain that I just didn't feel good. It wasn't exactly a lie. I knew I would never fit into whiteness. That was okay. But the loss of Blackness? I didn't know how to handle that. I was too white for Black people, and too Black for white people. I had a boy's name and bad acne. It was terrible.

Then, just when I thought I'd never fit anywhere, Blackness created space for me. I finally found a friend. Her name was Tiffani. She lived four houses down from my mother. We were the same age, but that and being Black were about all we had in common. She was short and spunky, self-confident and playful. I was tall but quiet, working hard at blending in. She was loud and cussed and taught me a few things about boys. She was everything I was not. She was everything I needed.

Whether she knew it or not, Tiffani became my teacher. She taught me about music and dances. She taught me about Ebonics and pop culture. She taught me about playing with neighborhood kids and running around outside until the streetlights came on. She danced with me. She played with me. And she vouched for me. She believed in my Blackness. And because she did, I could, too. To paraphrase the poet Ntozake Shange, there were no white girls in our hopscotch games.

Tiffani didn't just teach me about Black culture. She also taught me that I could embrace new things about Blackness without being stripped of my identity. I learned how to do the Butterfly—I almost won a dance contest that year, I'll have you know—but I also learned it was okay if I still preferred to read while everyone else played neighborhood kickball. I easily fell into Ebonics but never mastered the most popular slang, like *You buggin* or *Let's bounce;* it always sounded funny escaping my throat. I didn't see *Candyman* until I was grown.

Tiffani was my bridge to understanding that Black is beautiful whether it looked nerdy like me or cool like her. I could choose what felt right for me without needing to be like everyone, or needing everyone to be like me. Black is not monolithic. Black is expansive, and I didn't need the approval of whiteness in order to feel good in my skin; there was no whiteness available to offer an opinion. It was freedom.

I couldn't hear it when I first landed in Cleveland, but Blackness had been screaming (rather harshly, I'd thought), "There is another way." Another way of speaking, of thinking, of being that did not need white affirmation to be valuable. My way of speaking sounded like a hybrid of my white classmates and my Black parents, but that was not the only way to communicate. In fact, among the neighborhood kids, it wasn't the most valuable way to communicate. There was more than what I knew or could learn from a textbook; more than what whiteness said was right.

Lesson learned.

Summers in Cleveland weren't the only change I experienced as a result of my parents' divorce. Two years later, my dad remarried and my brother and I welcomed a new little sister into the world. Our family of five was creating new traditions, and on Sunday mornings we started going to church—a Black church in Toledo. Until this moment, all I knew of worship services were our school chapels on Friday afternoons. These usually consisted of [white] Christian contemporary songs, a passage read from our [white] illustrated Bibles, a [white] speaker sharing some sort of testimony, and finally accepting [white] Jesus as our Savior.

It was assumed by faculty, staff, and ultimately by most of the students that everything taking place in these chapel services applied to all bodies equally. I had no idea that when I walked into my dad's new church, I would be meeting black Jesus. I fell in love.

On that first Sunday, as we wandered down a fluorescent-lit hallway toward the sanctuary, the air was filled with the smell of perfume. I didn't know what to expect. Along the way congregation members welcomed us, the women in elaborate hats and dark stockings, the men in suits, ties, and snakeskin shoes. Everyone we passed greeted us with a warm *good morning* as if they already knew us. We waited a second at the wooden doors outside the sanctuary, because the people inside were in the middle of prayer. But soon, an "Amen" in unison filled the air, and the double doors swung open. Sunlight poured in from the stained glass windows lining the far wall. Pea green carpet stretched the length of the sanctuary. The organ had already started playing and everyone was standing on their feet, swaying the same direction. Hands clapped to the beat of the song.

I looked up into the choir stand, filled with brown faces like mine. The choir director moved her hands up and down in unison. Every member paid close attention to what she was doing. I later learned that this was because we rarely sang any song the same way twice. She wasn't just conducting prewritten music; she created a new song for us every time. We rewarded her with shouts of "Sing, choir!" and our own melody of "Hallelujahs."

That day, I fell in love. I fell in love with the soaring voices and the songs that moved us to tears and then chased the blues away. I fell in love with peppermint-dealing church mothers and hymn-singing deacons. I fell in love with fiery preaching that moved so deep, it would undergird you and push you to your feet in praise. I fell in love with a Jesus who saw the poor and sick and hurting, a Jesus who had bigger plans for me than keeping me a virgin, a Jesus who loved and reveled in our Blackness.

Sunday after Sunday, what grabbed my attention more than anything was the pastor. In sermons he preached, Jesus sounded like a Black person, dealing with familiar hardships of life—injustice, broken relationships, the pain of being called names. Pastor would read a passage of Scripture filled with *thee*s and *thou*s as beautiful as poetry. But then he would take the time to restate what happened to sound like the present day. He was incapable of standing still behind the pulpit—by the end of the service, he usually needed a face towel to wipe away the sweat from his forehead. But any given Sunday, the message was clear: *God was with us.*

We were a family. Sometimes dysfunctional, for sure. But we were constantly reminded of our connection to one another. We referred to each other as *brother* and *sister.* As we grew closer, those titles changed to *Auntie, Uncle,* even *Momma.*

I had to wait till adulthood before I heard the name James Cone or read about Black liberation theology. But by the time I learned of Black Jesus and his liberating power, I knew I had already met him at ten years old, in a Baptist church where the Spirit moved us every week. There Jesus cared about my soul, but he also cared about the woman who didn't have transportation or couldn't pay the light or water bill. Jesus cared about the folks who were addicted to drugs or alcohol, who wanted to save their bodies from the poison and their hearts from pain. And for those whose families hurt us, or significant others had left us, or supervisors didn't understand us—all these things were taken very seriously, but every Sunday we were also reminded that trouble don't last always. Heartbreak and struggle weren't the end of our story. We learned that God had some expectations for us, too, to resist sin and temptations of all kinds, but even these were offered contextualized—embodied, real in ways that the sermons from my school chapel services hadn't been.

The Black church gave me the greatest sense of belonging I had ever experienced. There was still much to learn: speaking in tongues, being slain in the Spirit, prophetic announcements and praise dances. (Not to mention, I hadn't realized that you could be in such a large group and everyone could clap in time on the two and four. Like, everyone . . .) It was an adjustment, but none of this made me nervous or uncomfortable like I'd been in school or during those first weeks in Cleveland. I loved the Black church and she loved me.

Slowly, over time and in layers, Blackness had found me. It found me and it changed my life.

3

The Other Side of Harmony

Much like my elementary school, the Catholic high school I attended was predominately white, but by then there were enough students of color to fill multiple tables at lunch, form a gospel choir, and generally make our presence known. To tell the truth, I don't remember any major racial incidents happening in any of the four years I was there. No swastikas on bathroom stalls, no fistfights prompted by an overconfident white boy using the n–word, no blackface parties or inappropriate Halloween costumes. For the most part, we all existed in harmony, but there were a few key moments in which I learned that *harmony*—the absence of outright conflict—often leaves deeper complications untouched.

Ms. Phillips's classroom was a favorite for students. She was short with a square frame and a foul mouth, which was intriguing since she taught our religion class. She mostly donned mom jeans and oversize shirts. She had a big laugh and told big stories, and as she taught from behind her podium, her energy filled the room.

Ms. Phillips gave us life lessons right alongside the curriculum (and sometimes *instead* of her curriculum). She told us about living in community with other single women, sharing resources, prioritizing friendships and intimacy. There was nothing we couldn't ask her. One day, after Ms. Phillips told us about her fear of ghosts, we stole the remote to the classroom TV and spent the class period turning it off and on. At first Ms. Phillips had us made, convinced we had figured out a way to control the television. But as the class wore on and the TV continued turning on and off, she started testing it. "If you are my uncle, turn off now," she countered. Off went the TV. She turned to us, eyes wide, and kept testing it by calling out the names of dead relatives. Minutes later, when we burst into laughter and revealed the truth, she wasn't mad at all. In fact, she dubbed us the best class she had ever had.

One day it was Ms. Phillips who caught us

off guard. As we filed into her classroom, she announced she would no longer use a seating chart. For the first time we scanned the room, deciding where we wanted to sit. Once we were settled, she informed us that she wanted to share why we suddenly had been given permission to choose our seats. There was something uncharacteristically soft about the way she spoke.

"Every year I use a seating chart," she began, "deciding where each of you will sit. Earlier this week I realized that my tendency to do this is racist." I froze. This was another classroom in which I was perhaps one of three students of color. I had no idea what was coming next, but I suddenly became very aware of my body.

"You see," she continued, "I have been using a seating chart to separate Black students. I didn't fully realize it until I failed to separate two Black young women in one of my classes. When I saw them together I panicked, thinking, *Great, now they are going to laugh and talk through the entire period.*"

She paused. She was clearly overwhelmed, yet making an effort to be as forthcoming as she would be about anything else. She did not mince words or sugarcoat any part of her thinking.

"That's when I realized what I was doing was racist. I have never ever wondered if any of my white students were going to be disruptive. I've never been nervous to find two white girls sitting next to one another. I am so disappointed with myself, and from now on, you all will sit where you want to sit."

She took a deep breath, and so did I. I'm guessing there were plenty of classes in which Ms. Phillips had to separate two white students for being disruptive. However, by her own admission, this tendency toward disruption was never attributed to their race. Only when the disruptive students were Black did race become a defining factor.

While I was grateful that she'd had an epiphany, or at least wanted to be grateful, the revelation made me incredibly self-conscious. I thought so much of Ms. Phillips; I wasn't prepared to hear what she had thought of me, of my body. The stereotype about sassy, disrespectful Black girls was not lost on me— but until then, I had thought it was just a convenient movie trope. I didn't realize it could be used against me.

I looked around the classroom to gauge the response of the other students. No one had much to add; I think most of them were just glad to be able to sit wherever they wanted. But I was having an entirely different experience. Should I have been glad for my teacher's aha moment? Did it make me safer in her classroom now that she was aware of her bias? What about the other teachers at my school? Were they—even the ones I liked—watching me, judging me?

It was the first time I saw beyond my own perception of the racial harmony at my school. I was grateful that I didn't have to deal with overt acts of racism, but was it better to know that teachers silently believed I would be a nuisance unless I proved otherwise? How could I know if beneath other amicable interactions, the stereotypes and biases of those in power were operating against students who looked like me?

This moment of disappointment made me even more determined to assert agency over my academic life. For the most part, my defiance manifested itself in demanding the right to explore Blackness. Book report due? I was choosing a Black author. History paper assigned? Black history was the only option for me. Like many Black students in predominately white schools, if I wanted to see myself reflected in the curriculum, I had to act on my own behalf.

Resisting an education built on a white worldview meant constantly having to evaluate the risks of telling the truth or furthering the myth. Would I write that Christopher Columbus "discovered" America? Would I do the report on Malcolm X instead of Mark Twain? My parents left the decision to me. I could choose the better grade or I could choose to affirm Blackness. It's a decision many students of color have to make. Sometimes I just stated the truth, "Christopher Columbus sailed the ocean blue in 1492, but the land he 'discovered' was already inhabited." Other times I would give the answer the teacher wanted with a disclaimer, "Our textbook states that . . ." I won't lie; I kind of enjoyed being more right than my teachers, even if it cost me half a letter grade.

So it was a rare gift when I could walk into a classroom that didn't require this kind of work from me. Mr. Slivinski's class was like that.

Mr. Slivinski was my freshman English teacher and the first to expose me to the power of an intentionally diverse curriculum. He was short, white, and full of energy—whether natural or from coffee, we couldn't tell. (He kept a warm pot in his classroom at all times.) On the first day of class, Mr. Sli informed us that his goal for the year was to give us a headache from thinking so hard. And he often succeeded. There were passionate discussions of Richard Connell's "The Most Dangerous

Game," line-by-line readings of Shakespeare, and assignments to analyze the character development in Daphne du Maurier's *Rebecca*. Through all of this, Mr. Slivinski inspired us to interrogate the assumptions we held about culture, ethics, laws. He wanted us to color outside the lines of our black and white thinking.

Mr. Slivinski's lesson plans would follow our textbook for a few weeks, and then break away for the sake of diversity. One of those breakaways was a unit on poetry. Each day, Mr. Slivinski printed out poems he'd selected, instructing us to read them and mark up the page. What words stood out? What did we notice about the structure? How did the content make us feel?

One day, Mr. Slivinski passed out a poem entitled "We Wear the Mask." I started reading immediately. The author's name, Paul Laurence Dunbar, was familiar to me. My stepmom worked as a high school English teacher and was always eager to recite Black poetry to me, so I knew we were about to read a poem about the Black experience. Still, my eyes widened as I read the words:

> *Why should the world be over-wise,*
> *In counting all our tears and sighs?*

Nay, let them only see us, while
We wear the mask.

A mask. My mind raced, wondering how often I did this without much thought. Were there parts of me that I kept buried from white people—even the ones I counted as friends? Things did feel different when I was the only Black girl in the class, versus when I was surrounded by Blackness at the lunch table or in our gospel choir. When I finished the poem, I felt both relieved and saddened. I looked up at Mr. Slivinski, wondering, *How do you know?*

When I realized he was about to open up the floor for discussion, I folded myself into the chair, trying to make my body smaller, trying to disappear. *Will you make me explain this? Will you ask me to tell this all-white class about the masks Black people wear?*

I was surprised by own reaction. It felt deeply gratifying to have my own experience named, lifted up, discussed, considered worthy of everyone's attention. And yet, I had no desire to be the Black spokesperson. It felt too risky. I wasn't sure that my classmates had earned the right to know, to understand, to be given access to such a vulnerable place in my experience. For me, this was more than an educational exercise. This is how we survive.

It's a common conundrum for Black children navigating mostly white classrooms. It is often expected—both by the other students and by the teacher—that Black students will have no problem acting as the race experts for their classrooms. Eventually, though, we begin to question whether we'll be safe when the subject comes up—or if we even have the right to speak on behalf of all Black people. I mean, it's not like we have a committee meeting every Wednesday night to decide what we think about any given issue. But my first reaction in this moment possessed none of these thoughts. I simply wasn't interested in taking off the mask.

Fortunately, Mr. Slivinski didn't call on me to respond to Dunbar's words. Though we had not exchanged one word since the exercise began, I sensed that he respected my decision to keep my thoughts private. I listened in amusement as white students—many of whom possessed an intellect and creativity that I sincerely admired—attempted to interpret the poem. No matter how well reasoned their responses, they just couldn't *know*. But that didn't stop Mr. Slivinski from challenging them.

I was grateful that my teacher was equipped to navigate that conversation without making me the momentary substitute teacher. Mr. Slivinski already had my respect, but that day, he also gained my trust. He was able to redraw the boundaries of our comfort zone. Breaking the social policy of just ignoring race didn't have to end badly. I wished he could steer discussions in every classroom.

I remember a religion class toward the end of my senior year when our teacher asked the students about our future plans. Most of us were bound for college in the fall, so the conversation gravitated toward talk of applications, scholarships, and possible majors—a discussion that led one white classmate to air her grievances about not being accepted to the University of Michigan. Rather than chalking it up to the sheer number of applications U of M must receive in any given year, she had a different explanation: A Black person must have taken her place. And not a Black person who perhaps had above-average test scores, who'd completed more hours of community service, or perhaps had written a stronger biographical essay on the application. Had this been her assumption about the Black people who earned spots at the university, I probably could have forgiven her. But alas, her explanation was short: "Because of affirmative action, Black people took my spot."

Her spot.

Or, if I were to add all that was left unspoken in her sentence: "If the University of Michigan hadn't let unqualified Black people in, I, who am obviously deserving and qualified above and beyond those people, would have easily been accepted."

My blood boiled. I really wanted to hurt her feelings. I wanted to suggest that perhaps she was not as qualified as *any* of the students who were let in—Black or otherwise. I wanted to tell her that if I was one of the applicants, I knew for a fact I would get in before her, and it had nothing to do with my skin color. I wanted to tell her that no one stole anything from her; that's what made it an application.

My reaction surprised me. I had not applied to U of M, and yet her words stung as if I had personally offended her with access to the coveted university. In my mind, she wasn't just talking about a specific group of Black students. She was talking about Black people, all of us. That's why I wanted to hurt her feelings. She was telling me exactly what she thought about Black people, and I was ready to tell her about herself in return.

Back then I didn't have all the terminology I have now to process awkward interactions with white people. I didn't have phrases like *white tears* or *white fragility,* and I'm not sure I had even explored the term *white privilege* at that point in my life. But I was learning about these things all the same—not from theory, but from life.

Our teacher completely froze as the tension climbed. But more concerning was that four years at a racially diverse school hadn't been enough to challenge my classmate's belief that whiteness, on its own merit, made her more deserving. Our school's "racial harmony" might not have created that assumption, but it didn't help her unlearn it either. A lack of confrontation had done her no favors. As high school came to an end, I took this lesson with me and became determined always to question what looks like unity at first glance.

4

Ain't No Friends Here

By the time I went off to college, Chicago seemed like the perfect place to practice adulthood. The city took my breath away. The fast pace, the gorgeous architecture, the diversity at every turn. It seemed to me that important things were happening here.

When I walked onto campus my freshman year, my first surprise was Crendalyn McMath. She was my first Black teacher, a marketing professor, and she took command of every classroom she stepped into. Tall with shoulder-length black hair, she wore suits that seemed only to elongate her frame. She was a brilliant teacher who brought stories from her professional experience into the classroom. I was so proud that she was a Black woman, like me.

The gift of Professor McMath's presence went

beyond the fact that she looked like me, though that was special all by itself. The true gift was that I didn't have to create my own sense of belonging in her class. In every previous classroom, I had been responsible for decoding teachers' references to white middle-class experiences. *It's like when you're sailing . . .* or *You know how when you're skiing, you have to . . .* My white teachers had an unspoken commitment to the belief that *we are all the same,* a default setting that masked for them how often white culture bled into the curriculum. For example, when teachers wanted to drive home the point that we should do something daily, they often likened it to how you wash your hair every morning. It never occurred to them that none of the Black girls in the class did this. Knowing it was true for white people, and having gotten used to white teachers' assumption of universality, we would all nod our heads and move on. Who had time to teach the teacher?

But Professor McMath was different. One day, while illustrating a point regarding business planning, she decided to use the example of opening a beauty shop. Our conversation moved along as usual until Professor McMath made an analogy to "getting a relaxer." My head snapped up in recognition, but all the white students looked toward the lectern completely baffled. I was the only one who understood the reference. I smiled at Professor McMath while she feigned surprise at the other students' confusion. "Come on, you all. You know what a relaxer is, right?" They continued to stare blankly at her until she explained that some Black women choose to get a relaxer, which is sort of the opposite of what happens when white people get a perm. "Relaxers make black curly hair straight . . . they relax the curls." She winked at me, and I grinned from ear to ear.

I relished the sense of belonging I felt in her classroom. Suddenly I wasn't content to feel like I was attending a college made for someone else. I paid tuition like every white student. Something was stirring inside, and there was one particular experience that caused it to burst out in full.

That spring, my roommate invited me on a trip called Sankofa. Sankofa was a three-day journey down South exploring Black history in partnership with another student. There were about twenty pairs of us, mostly comprising one Black and one white student. We traveled all night long from Chicago to Louisiana, arriving at our first stop: a plantation.

We had come prepared to witness the harsh realities of slavery, but the real revelation was how ignorant and self-congratulatory our guides from the plantation could be. For the entire tour, we were told about "happy slaves" who sang in the fields, who worked under better conditions than most other slaves, and whose fingers never bled despite the massive amounts of cotton they picked. The guides' presentations were filled with misconceptions and inaccuracies, and at the conclusion of the tour, they even gave us the chance to pick some cotton ourselves.

Black students. Picking cotton.

The anger of the Black students and the confusion of the white students was palpable. As we climbed aboard the bus to roll to our next destination, our conversation quickly moved beyond superficial niceties. We took turns speaking into a microphone at the front of the bus. The Black students were livid at the romanticism displayed at the plantation. The white students listened politely but seemed unmoved as they weighed our information against the "experts" at the plantation. They responded with questions like "What about the Holocaust or the potato famine? Don't most people groups have some trauma in their history?" We did our best to correct the misconceptions, but the tour had driven a wedge in the group. And our next stop would drive that wedge even deeper.

Our bus pulled in to a museum consisting of only one exhibit—a history of lynching. Every wall was filled with photographs of dark-skinned human beings swinging by their necks. A mother and son hanging over a bridge. Burned bodies swinging over dying fires. White children staring in wide-eyed wonder while their parents proudly point to the mutilated body behind them. The cruel smiles of white faces testifying to the joy of the occasion. We came across newspaper stories that advertised lynchings as community events. In another case we saw a postcard. On the front was a photo of a mutilated man still hanging from a rope. On the other side, a handwritten note: "Sorry we missed you at the barbecue."

There was no sound as we walked through the exhibit. We could barely breathe, let alone speak.

When we climbed back on the bus, all that could be heard were sniffles. The emotion was thick. It was as if no time had passed between the generation in the pictures and the one sitting on that bus. It was all so real.

The first students to break the silence were white. "I didn't know this even happened." "It's not my fault; I wasn't there." They reached for anything that would distance themselves from the pain and anger of the moment; anything to ward off the guilt and shame, the shock and devastation.

The Black students had passed beyond any need to appear polite. We shared personal stories of pain—lynchings that happened to our own families—trying to make real those bodies from the photographs. But we weren't just interested in focusing on Black bodies; we were going to focus on white ones, too.

A tall Black woman, a senior that year, peered at us all as she spoke evenly, almost disarmingly in the heat of the moment. "I just want to say that I'm having a hard time even being mad at you white people anymore. I think I've just been convinced that white people are innately evil. You can't help it. You steal and kill, you enslave and lynch. You are just evil." Then she handed the microphone back to the next person and calmly took her seat. The white students hadn't appreciated her words, but the Black students on the bus could have kissed her feet. She had done what social convention and respectability politics said not to do—she had spoken her truth even if it meant hurting the feelings of every white person on that bus.

The tension climbed. Black and white grew further and further apart with each new speaker. The white students defended their family histories as the Black students searched for the words to express how it felt to stare at ours in those photos from the museum. Then, as we pulled into a parking lot to break for lunch, another white student stood to speak. But instead of a different variation on "Please don't make me responsible for this," she took a deep breath and gave in to the emotion of it all.

"I don't know what to do with what I've learned," she said. "I can't fix your pain, and I can't take it away, but I can see it. And I can work for the rest of my life to make sure your children don't have to experience the pain of racism."

And then she said nine words that I've never forgotten: "Doing nothing is no longer an option for me."

Those words changed the air on that bus. She acknowledged the depth of our pain without making excuse for it. And in that moment, I knew her words were true for me as well. Something shifted inside me on this trip. Something powerful and unmistakable. Doing nothing was no longer an option for me.

Sankofa was the first time I felt the distance

between history and myself collapsing. The black-and-white photos I had grown used to were now filled with color, associated with real places, places I had now walked. The inspiration to be part of their legacy was palpable, and the ways Christianity had been used to uphold all the evil of this history was not lost on me. Somehow, I just knew it was time to devote myself to the struggle.

After many more stops, discussions, tears, and prayers, we returned home. But before we got off the bus, our leaders had one final task for us. We all had to share one way in which we would become change agents as a result of the trip. I don't remember what I said that day, but my commitment was genuine.

I was no organizer, like many of my girlfriends on that trip. But I did start showing up. I helped challenge our college's administration to hire and retain Black faculty and staff. I attended race-related events like movie discussions and conferences, lending my voice to the cause. I started small gatherings where diversity could be practiced—prayer groups and worship services. Unlike in high school, where I noticed racism but kept my thoughts to myself, in college I started speaking up.

Our college was white, so most students of color

found themselves constantly teaching white folks about racial justice. For the most part we embraced this role. Finally, people saw *us* as the experts in the room. We enjoyed asserting ourselves, our history, our culture, in a space that was dominated by the normalization of whiteness. In our minds, we were fighting the good fight. But I must confess: These first collegiate attempts at seeking racial justice were a little unhealthy.

Somewhere along the way, I picked up the unspoken belief that I was made for white people. That might sound weird, but it's true. Much of my teaching (and learning) managed to revolve around whiteness—white privilege, white ignorance, white shame, the things white folks "needed" in order to believe racial justice is a worthy cause. Movie discussions on *Do the Right Thing* or *Crash* often focused on the white characters, and "privilege walks" focused on making white people recognize the unearned advantages they'd gotten at birth.

I worked as if white folks were at the center, the great hope, the linchpin, the key to racial justice and reconciliation—and so I contorted myself to be the voice white folks could hear. It's amazing how white supremacy even invades programs aimed at seeking racial reconciliation. Just when I was about to lose myself to whiteness in an entirely different way, along came the second Black teacher of my life.

Dr. Simms taught courses in African American and Mexican American history. Brown, bald, and bespectacled, he wore clothes from Phat Farm and had a small leather pouch that he strapped like a messenger bag across the front of his chest. Standing no taller than five foot seven, but commanding a gravitas that many students found intimidating, the man was an intellectual powerhouse and possessed a wealth of experience that kept him grounded in real life. Many of the white students avoided him like the plague, but I didn't know a Black student who would dare graduate without taking at least one of his classes. Dr. Simms believed in the power of Black history and Black culture. He believed it could change our lives.

Dr. Simms was right.

He began each class period with a list of new terms written on the chalkboard—one of which was usually spelled incorrectly. We often teased him for being so brilliant that he didn't have space in his brain for such trivial matters as spelling. For a class period focusing on slavery in America, we would arrive with Dr. Simms's terms already on the board: *chattel, Middle Passage, slave codes, rebellion, Dred Scott,* and five or six more phrases. He would then spend the period defining each one in narrative form, making us feel like we'd witnessed events of the past.

As he taught, Dr. Simms spoke softly and repetitiously, making sure we understood his point. But he also wanted to know what we thought. "Tell me, Kate, what do you think about that?" Dr. Simms would ask. If someone spoke too softly or too hesitantly, he would extend his index and middle fingers together, twirling them in the air as he encouraged the student. "Speak up. We want to hear what you have to say. Speak up so those in the back can hear you." It didn't matter whether our insights were profound or middling—Dr. Simms always found a way to incorporate our ideas into his lecture. His gentleness did not stop him from demanding that we think deeply.

Dr. Simms wanted us to be suspicious of the language of America.

He taught us to analyze the news. Did anyone notice how only the faces of Black criminals were shown in this segment? In the next segment, the anchor said there was a crowd—could you tell if the camera angle made it seem larger or smaller?

That whole story was on immigrants, but why did it focus only on immigrants of color? He wanted us to pay attention. I remember him often bringing in multiple newspapers—one the English-language *Chicago Tribune* and the other *Hoy*, the Spanish-language paper headquartered in the same city. He would have us read two stories on the same topic, then ask, "How are these two stories different? What details did the *Trib* leave out or *Hoy* include?"

He also encouraged us to question everyday "patriotic" language. When referring to the drafters of the Constitution, Dr. Simms refused to call them the Founding Fathers. "Those aren't my Fathers!" he would state matter-of-factly. His declaration invited the question for the rest of us: *Are they mine?*

We always told Dr. Simms that he ruined our lives. He made us so aware of racial bias, we could no longer watch the news as leisure. We analyzed movies for accuracy like we never had before. Newly conscious that the literature we read carried an angle, we now couldn't help but seek it out. We thought critically about everything, and it was all Dr. Simms's fault.

Dr. Simms didn't just make us recite names and dates. He taught us to care about the past. When he spoke of Martin Luther King Jr.'s assassination, his eyes would fill with tears. It was like he was hearing the announcement all over again. He wept so hard after showing a documentary on the work of Cesar Chavez, he had to dismiss class that day. Dr. Simms wanted us to be emotionally connected to our learning, to sit in the pain, the horror, the absurdity of America's racist history, and to humanize those who dared stand against the system. Dr. Simms made us believe that we could follow that legacy of resistance, but one piece of his advice stood out to me more than all the others.

"Ain't no friends here."

Whenever Dr. Simms said this—in a lecture on Lincoln's true views on race, or while talking about the mainstream media's mixed track record in covering social movements—it always made me laugh. Dr. Simms wouldn't hurt a fly. He exuded gentleness and softness, and he relied on knowledge and humor when responding to critics. I never heard him raise his voice to anyone except to shout "Friends! Friends!" when our discussions became incomprehensible with passion. So hearing him say anything that could be perceived as an overgeneralization or inherently suspicious of others seemed like a departure. And yet, we all knew he was not joking. We already had plenty of examples in our history books and on our college campus, but it would take some time to figure out how deep and wide his life lesson would stretch.

For the rest of undergrad, my professor's words would come back to me whenever white people acted a fool. When they wrote in our newspaper that the Black students should just leave if we weren't happy. When I overheard racist comments in the cafeteria, or explained to the residence director for the millionth time that our lobby isn't suddenly "scary" when Black football players happen to be occupying it. Any time something like this happened, Dr. Simms's voice would sound in my head: *Ain't no friends here.*

Professor McMath, Dr. Simms, and a handful of additional faculty and staff members helped me define what it meant to be a Black student in white spaces. They helped me demand what I wanted. They made it safe for me to explore my own voice. Though I was often surrounded by whiteness, they reminded me that I was capable of responding to racist white people, and encouraged me to seek comfort in Black history and the healing of Black community. They pushed me to rethink what whiteness had taught me about myself, about my personhood, about my vocation, about my place in the world. They were teaching me to speak up until those in the back could hear me.

School was over. Time for the real world. Turned out Dr. Simms was right, even when I didn't want him to be.

5

Whiteness at Work

Confession: By the time I graduated from college, I thought I was the white culture whisperer. I was fearless. I thought any future encounters of racism would rear their ugly heads like purple dragons, and I had no doubt in my ability to slay racist nonsense wherever I found it. I was so wrong. Far from an imposing beast, I found that white supremacy is more like a poison. It seeps into your mind, drip by drip, until it makes you wonder if your perception of reality is true.

Being a Black woman in the professional world of majority-white nonprofit ministries was far more difficult than my younger self could imagine. In school I had been surrounded by whiteness, but colleges often encourage students to question authority, to navigate cultural conflicts, to be creative

in starting alternative organizations and clubs.
While every school certainly contains boundaries
for students, at some basic level it is expected that
students push those boundaries, that they learn not
only through books but through new experiences.
The professional world, I soon discovered, is altogether different.

Companies love talking about their "diversity
and inclusion efforts," but I remember one unusu-
ally frank conversation with our organization's
board of directors, in which I learned how those
efforts often work. Less than a year into the job,
I was seeking approval for a new racial diversity
training program. I knew the meeting wasn't going
well when the treasurer said, "Just to play devil's
advocate . . ." and then posed a series of questions,
speaking gently so as to preserve an air of innocence. "Why don't we want assimilation? Isn't that
the point of an organization's culture? Don't we
want to bring in people of diverse backgrounds and
then become one unified organization?"

My mouth dropped open, but the rest of my
body froze. I had no idea how to speak truth to the
person who held my program in his hands. How
could I possibly explain that the unity he desired
always came at my expense? I had worked for a

number of organizations that struggled to create meaningful opportunities for people of color, but I had never heard anyone make an overt case in favor of assimilation—particularly at an organization that promoted diversity in its mission statements and messaging. Granted, many people of color on our team had grown suspicious of those statements, suspecting that the organization wanted our racial diversity without our diversity of thought and culture. I just never imagined someone with his influence would say it aloud and with positivity.

It's so easy to believe the pretty pictures on the website filled with racial diversity, to buy in to the well-crafted statements of purpose, to enjoy being invited into the process of "being part of the change." The role of a bridge builder sounds appealing until it becomes clear how often that bridge is your broken back.

It usually begins with the job interview.

Overcompensation is hard to resist in this moment. When you need a job, and are genuinely drawn to the work described in the job posting, it's tempting to sit in that seat and say all the right things, laugh the right laugh, extend all the right jokes. The goal, after all, is to impress. Do I make myself more likable? Do I use references to movies, music, books that I know the folks around the table would appreciate—references that would imply *I am just like you*? Sometimes I just want to prove I can do it. That I can make them comfortable, make them believe. But the question is always, *Is it worth it?*

White institutions are constantly communicating how much Blackness they want. It begins with numbers. How many scholarships are being offered? How many seats are being "saved" for "neighborhood kids"? How many Black bodies must be present for us to have "good" diversity numbers? How many people of color are needed for the website, the commercials, the pamphlets?

But numbers are only the beginning. Whiteness constantly polices the expressions of Blackness allowed within its walls, attempting to accrue no more than what's necessary to affirm itself. It wants us to sing the celebratory "We Shall Overcome" during MLK Day but doesn't want to hear the indicting lyrics of "Strange Fruit." It wants to see a Black person seated at the table but doesn't want to hear a dissenting viewpoint. It wants to pat itself on the back for helping poor Black folks through missions or urban projects but has no interest in learning from Black people's wisdom, talent, and spiritual depth. Whiteness wants enough Blackness to affirm the goodness of whiteness, the progressiveness of whiteness, the openheartedness of whiteness. Whiteness likes a trickle of Blackness, but only that which can be controlled.

Here's how all of this plays out if you're a Black woman trying to survive in a culture of professional whiteness:

8:55 A.M.: I arrive at work and walk through the lobby to get to my office. On the way, I am asked three times if I need help finding the outreach center. My white co-worker, whose footsteps I hear behind me, is never asked this question. *The message: I am a Black woman, so I must be poor and in need of help.*

8:58 A.M.: I set my purse down in my cubicle. The white co-worker who was walking behind me stares in shock. She has never seen me with my hair in a pineapple fro. She reaches out to touch my hair while telling me how beautiful it is. When I pull back, startled by the sudden act of intimacy, she looks hurt and isn't sure what to do next. *The message: I am different, exotic. Anyone should have the right to my body in exchange for a compliment.*

9:58 A.M.: An hour later, I am asked to see my supervisor. When I get to her office she asks me to shut the door. She tells me she received a note saying that I made someone uncomfortable when they were just trying to be friendly and kind. She suggests that I work on being more of a team player, and not being so closed off. I look at her incredulously. I now wonder if this is just about the one co-worker, or if my supervisor gets emails about me every week from awkward white people. *The message: I am responsible for the feelings of white people, and my boss will not defend me from these accusations.*

10:05 A.M.: I attempt to respond, but before I can finish, my supervisor asks if I don't mind changing my tone a bit. I sound angry and she was trying to be helpful, trying to make sure I can stay here long-term. I mumble something about my own frustrations, but they are dismissed with a wave of her hand and a promise to work with me. *The message: My tone will be interpreted as angry, even if I'm just feeling hurt or misunderstood. My actual feelings are irrelevant and could be used as reason to fire me.*

12:00 noon: It's lunchtime now, and I desperately need to talk to my girlfriends in another department. I find a seat among this group of women of color who use the lunch break to offer support and encouragement to one another. After talking with them for a little bit, I feel like I can breathe again. Even though we don't work in the same departments, they are the reason I've survived here this long. I return to my office.

1:00 P.M.: I have a project due at the end of the week, so I put on my headphones to block out the office noise while I work. Another team member comes to my door. "Austin, can I talk to you for a second?" "Sure," I respond. "I noticed that you wear your headphones a lot in the office," she says. "It sometimes feels like you don't want to be around us." I take a deep breath. Because we work in cubicles, many of us wear headphones when we need to focus. Mine aren't on more often than anyone else's. *The message: My body is being scrutinized in ways that others are not subjected to, and the worst is being assumed of me.*

1:05 P.M.: I respond to the co-worker but quickly turn the conversation to the project we're working on together, hoping to discuss the changes I made that morning. Thirty minutes into this conversation, I realize I am answering questions about Black music, a news segment on "urban violence" she saw the other night, and something her adopted Black nephew said the other day. She emphasizes the word *black,* clearly not used to saying the word. I am tired. I am not sure what led us here. *The message: I am here to educate my white co-workers when they are confused about a racial issue in their lives.*

1:40 P.M.: I take a deep breath. "Hey, I need to stretch my legs. I'm going to get some coffee, you want anything?" I don't like coffee, but I will get some anyway if it helps end this conversation.

1:50 P.M.: Standing in line at the coffee shop next door, I quickly notice a man who stopped me in the hallway and referred to me as "colored." He had come to one session of my Tuesday night class on race and thought it appropriate to pepper me with questions about Blackness (well, "colored-ness") since he'd decided not to continue coming. Rather than answer his questions on the spot, I'd told him he should come back to the class. But now here he is behind me. Maybe he won't speak up, or maybe he'll think he has me confused with another Black person. He doesn't say anything, but my body is stiff with anticipatory tension.

2:07 P.M.: As soon as I get my coffee and turn toward the door, it happens. Someone I have never met insists that she emailed me and can't wait to chat more. She is right that we work at the same organization, but I've never seen this woman. "I think you have me confused with someone else," I say.

She insists I am wrong. "Oh no, don't you remember . . ." I stare at her blankly, my warm coffee reminding me that I am not in the sunken place.

I let her finish, then I repeat slowly, "I think you have me confused with someone else." The explanation continues until I am given enough information to know which Black person she has me confused with. "Nope, that's not me. You're talking about Tina in the communications department. She is amazing, you two will have a good talk, I'm sure." Her eyes grow wide, embarrassment climbing her face. "I'm so sorry, I have to run!" I say, before the apologies get messy. *The message: My body, my person is not distinct; I am interchangeable with all other Black women.*

2:17 P.M.: I'm back in my office; preparing for an afternoon staff meeting in which I will give a short presentation. I feel good about my content— I've worked hard on it, knowing my perspective is often different from my co-workers'—but my heart still beats fast. How will I be received by my team?

2:30 P.M.: I'm in the staff meeting. I give my eight-minute spiel. There is a pause, and then some pushback. I knew this was a possibility, so I hear them out, trying not to form a response as they speak. Another co-worker pipes in before I can respond: "I think what Austin is trying to say is . . ." Suddenly everyone is nodding in agreement even though I'm pretty sure she repeated me almost word for word. *The message: I need white approval and interpretation before my idea will be considered good.*

3:30 P.M.: The meeting has closed, and some co-workers race back to their cubicles. Even though I am behind on emails, I know that I must stay and chat. If I race back to my cubicle it will be interpreted as me being antisocial. I stick around and make small talk, leaving with another co-worker so that my body doesn't stand out.

3:40 P.M.: I'm back in my office. I glance at the clock. There are still two more hours in the day.

These are the daily annoyances, the subtle messages of whiteness. But we bear other scars, too. Over and over I have seen white men and women get praise for their gifts and skills while women of color are told only about their *potential* for leadership. When white people end up being terrible at their jobs, I have seen supervisors move mountains to give them new positions more suited to their talents, while people of color are told to master their positions or be let go. I have been in the room when promises were made to diversify boardrooms, leadership teams, pastoral staff, faculty and staff positions, only to watch committees appoint a white man in the end. It's difficult to express how these

incidents accumulate, making you feel underval-
ued, unappreciated, and ultimately expendable.

Over the years, I have grown used to hearing
the response "Well, why don't you just leave if you
don't like it here?" As if this experience is a unique
phenomenon, or specific to only a handful of de-
linquent organizations. Even if it were unique, it's
highly privileged to believe that Black women can
just quit and find another place to work without
missing paychecks or losing benefits. Just changing
jobs is rarely that simple. So Black women come up
with life hacks.

These life hacks don't involve nifty uses for egg
cartons or finding unique ways to use paper clips.
They involve helping one another write emails to
our supervisors or coworkers, which we know will
be scrutinized for tone. Our life hacks include keeping folders in our in-boxes where we place every
single email that praises our project, attitude, or
giftedness. This is not for our self-esteem; it's an in-
surance policy, because we know there are emails
being sent to our bosses that say the opposite. Our
life hacks include finding a cohort, a girlfriend, an
ally—someone who is safe. Someone to have lunch
with who doesn't need an explanation of our being.
Our life hacks include secret Facebook groups

where we process awkward interpersonal microaggressions and suggest ways to tackle them in the future.

But for many of us, life hacks can't stop the inevitable. They can slow it down, yes. But eventually, those of us who work for white Christians are asked the question *Are you sure God has really called you . . . here?*

And then I know just how invisible and dispensible I am.

Rather than having a conversation about policy or assumptions or interactions, I am asked what God thinks about me. This is convenient, because it allows the people in charge to wash their hands of the conflict. But the suggestion that I assimilate doesn't always come passive-aggressively, or with ill intent. Sometimes it sounds loving.

It's been a hard week at the office. Because I work at a Christian organization, my co-workers ask if they can pray for me. I am moved that they've noticed my emotional distress. They gather round, lay their hands on my shoulders. I close my eyes and breathe deeply, listening to their words. But before I know it, the prayers take a turn. They are no longer about my circumstances but about me. They ask not that I would be understood but that

I would find it within myself to give more grace. The prayers don't ask that doors would open for me; they ask that God would gift me with skills they wish I had. These prayers aren't for me. The prayers are that I would become who *they* want me to be. "Lord, make this Black person just like us."

I'm not sure my co-workers even realize the difference; they've been praying the prayer for so long. In this way whiteness reveals its true desire for people of color. Whiteness wants us to be empty, malleable, so that it can shape Blackness into whatever is necessary for the white organization's own success. It sees potential, possibility, a future where Black people could share some of the benefits of whiteness if only we try hard enough to mimic it. The initial expectation is that I simply code-switch, conforming to the cultural communication of white people when I'm with them. But in the end, this is never enough. The ultimate expectation is that I will come to realize that white ways of thinking, behaving, communicating, and understanding the world are to be valued above all else.

Rare is the ministry praying that they would be worthy of the giftedness of Black minds and hearts. So we must remind ourselves. It's the only way to spit out the poison. We must remind ourselves and one another that we are fearfully and wonderfully made, arming ourselves against the ultimate message of whiteness—that we are inferior. We must stare at ourselves in the mirror and repeat that we, too, are fully capable, immensely talented, and uniquely gifted. We are not tokens. We are valuable in the fullness of our humanity. We are not perfect, but we are here, able to contribute something special, beautiful, lasting to the companies and ministries to which we belong.

Interlude:

Why I Love Being a Black Girl

As a Black woman working in white spaces, my perception of racial dynamics has been questioned, minimized, or denied altogether. Over time, the experience of not being believed, especially by people I thought were my friends, wore away my sense of self. As I entered the professional world and sensed this happening to me, it became vital to remind myself daily of why I love being a Black girl:

I am enlivened by our stories of survival. Even though white folks tried to steal our histories—our lives, our labor, our culture, our origins—we recover the records. We find the census, the photos, the certificates, the inscriptions. Thanks to my grandmother, I am filled with stories of triumph over slavery, over lynching, over Jim Crow, because our dignity was too strong to crush. I have felt the cast-iron pot of my grandmother and held the Bible of my great-grandmother. I sit at the feet of my elders and listen to them honor our shared past.

When I begin to doubt myself, I remember that we are creators. We are pioneers of language itself. We invent new words and kill old ones. We smash syllables together and watch them reverberate across the nation. We have a language we share with one another. Though our words are stolen and often misused or misapplied, we know the depth of our vocabulary when used among ourselves. Our conversations are call-and-response. Someone uncolored might assume we are cutting each other off, interrupting—but all we did was move church outside the building walls. We will shout "Yes, amen" and "You better say that" in affirmation of one another.

When my body stands out and I am tempted to forget my own beauty, I close my eyes and remember the feel of my father's fingers against my scalp, braiding each perfectly parted row while telling me I am not tender-headed so stop squirming. There was the cooling sensation of Blue Magic and Pink Lotion and the smell of hot curling irons as I learned about all the special things my hair can do.

Natural or relaxed, braided or dreaded, twisted or knotted, cornrowed or weaved—our hair believes in being free to do what she wants. When I rub cocoa butter into my skin, I remember the warmth of my mother's hands when she used to tell me to get all the hidden spots—behind my ankles and around my knees. The memories of her care for my body are a reminder of the care my body deserves.

Black women are the backbone and muscle of every church I've attended. They are prophets speaking a word when it seems God is silent. They are hospitality, welcoming with food and kindness, with a seat at the table, with a place you can call home. We are capable of building community anywhere—not just at church or at work, but also in the "ethnic" hair care section of stores, in elevators, and other random places where we take the opportunity to simply say, "I see you."

I love being a Black woman because we are demanding. We demand the right to live as fully human. We demand access—the right to vote, to education, to employment, to housing, to equal treatment under the law. And we do it creatively: Sit-ins and die-ins, signs and songs, writing and filmmaking. We demand because our ancestors did. We demand because we believe in our own dignity.

I could go on and on. I haven't touched the poetry of Nikki Giovanni, Lucille Clifton, and every southern grandmother who ever urged her children to keep on keeping on. I haven't covered the hugs and head nods and compliments from strangers; the Black cool of our photographers and dancers, politicians and teachers, and the everyday folks we love. There is so much beauty to share. But my point is this: I love being a Black girl.

6

White Fragility

A lot of white people have never sat under the authority of a Black teacher, pastor, professor, or supervisor. The person who's in control, setting the standards, handing out the grades, making the moral commands, is usually someone who looks like them. As I grew into my career and found myself in positions of relative authority, I learned that being the first Black woman authority figure in a white person's world can be . . . intense.

I'll never forget the day when one white man in particular made it clear for me how combustible white folks can be. I had just finished teaching a class called Race and Faith. We spent the class period discussing common racial stereotypes, where they come from, how they are reinforced, and what we can do to combat them in ourselves and others.

Toward the end of our time together, I pointed to the far wall, still covered in Post-its from the activity, recounting the aha moments of our discussion. The participants sat in a large circle in folding chairs, but I noticed one man sat with his arms crossed, sinking down into his chair, clearly brooding over the content of our class. As I spoke, he attempted to interrupt me, but I asked him if he wouldn't mind waiting until the class was over. I could tell by his body language and the heat in his voice that he was not interested in engaging so much as fighting, but I hoped listening to one of my co-teachers end the class with Scripture and prayer would help him calm down. It didn't work.

Minutes after my co-teacher said amen, officially ending the class, the man stood across a high-top table, screaming at me. His face had turned entirely red. He stood a head taller than me, and his eyes were wide as he waved his outstretched hands in my face. His voice alternated between passionate debate and outright exasperation.

I looked at the faces of my co-teachers to make sure this scene was as over the top as it felt to me. "Trayvon Martin is not a victim," he yelled. He then pointed to the Post-its on the wall where the other participants had confessed their association of the word *thug* with Black people. He attempted to school me. "Black boys just need jobs. That's it. Do you know the jobless rate of Black boys?" As he circled through these points again and again, I struggled to understand what any of this had to do with me. All we knew was that I had become the object of his anger. The eyes of my co-teachers, wide with disbelief, said it all, "Yep, this is unreal."

I placed my hands on the table between myself and the man, willing myself toward emotional stability. The louder his voice became, the more I dropped mine. Still, for the next twenty minutes, he raged at me, teaching me everything he thought he knew about Black boys in the hood. When it became clear that I was already pretty familiar with the topic, he pivoted. "Who is really in charge here?" At last, we had arrived at the true source of this conflict: my incompetence. Surely someone else, someone occupying a different body, would understand him.

A white male co-worker, offended at this question, stepped in. "Austin is in charge here. This is her class. But would you mind talking with me over here, if that's okay with you, Austin?" I nodded, appreciating the request for permission. The pair walked to the other side of the classroom, while

I attempted to regroup from the onslaught of the man's temper.

His wife—small and quiet—happened to be in the group that was listening. "I'm so sorry," she said to me. "He came in late, missing all the setup, the activity, and half the discussion. When he came in, you mentioned Trayvon Martin and he saw the Post-its from the activity on the wall naming the stereotypes faced by Black boys. The combination just set him off."

Well, that's annoying. And sadly, it's all too common for qualified Black women to find themselves facing off with white ignorance. White men have yelled at me in defensiveness, challenged the entirety of my talks during open Q and A sessions, and simply ignored me as if I don't exist, gathering all their privilege like a shield. White women have dismissed me completely, crumbled into tears, or launched into stories that center on That One Time Something Bad Happened to Them. Beneath the volatility, the combativeness, white people become disturbed because they often can't fathom Black people have something important to teach them about themselves and about the world.

That day I cried. I knew I had done nothing wrong, but my body was still processing the onslaught of anger and condescension. I willed my body to relax, removing my hands from the table and crossing them in front of my chest, a feeble attempt to stop from shaking. I knew more than that man did about all the things he considered himself an expert on—Black boys, the hood, the nonprofits working on issues of crime, poverty, and education. But instead of recognizing that I am flesh, blood, emotion, real, a human, he had taken all these things for granted, speaking to me in a way that he wouldn't have to anyone who looked like him.

This is partly what makes the fragility of whiteness so damn dangerous. It ignores the personhood of people of color and instead makes the feelings of whiteness the most important thing. It happens in classes and workshops, board meetings and staff meetings, via email and social media, but it takes other forms, too. If Black people are dying in the street, we must consult with white feelings before naming the evils of police brutality. If white family members are being racist, we must take Grandpa's feelings into account before we proclaim our objections to such speech. If an organization's policies are discriminatory and harmful, that can only be corrected if we can ensure white people won't feel bad about the change. White fragility protects whiteness and forces Black people to fend for themselves.

The day after the man raged at me, I was pulled

into a meeting by a staff member. Several of my co-teachers, both Black and white, started by re-hashing the events. But before I knew it, the conversation became about the feelings of the white man and what I could have done to calm him down. Perhaps if I had let him walk it off or traveled to a different location in the room. Perhaps if I had used a different, friendlier tone. Perhaps if I had done something magically obvious, something simple—something they surely would have done—maybe the white man would have been less irate, less threatening toward me.

This conversation was not about my safety, my security, my authority. Not about my feelings, but about his. About how I should have taken care of those feelings, changed those feelings so that I would have been safe.

No one was yelling or threatening me physically. In fact, everyone present loved me, yet white fragility was undergirding this conversation, too. I was pretty sure that if the man had treated a white woman this way, we'd be having a different discussion. This meeting was not for my support; it was a critique. But just when I was starting to wonder if my own co-workers would indulge my humanity, someone spoke up. "Wait a second," she said. "This conversation seems to have moved away from the reality that this grown man is responsible for his own feelings. And there is no circumstance under which his behavior would be tolerated if used against any other teacher or speaker. Austin did nothing wrong."

The group began to backtrack, looking at me in horror as if I'd been the one who'd chided them. But the conversation shifted. They stopped focusing on what I could have done differently and began discussing how the church could protect me and the other women leading the class. Feeling emboldened, I made it clear that a class on race, led by a Black woman, would likely draw similar reactions in the future.

I am grateful the conversation moved forward, but it reminded me how easy it is to center white feelings without thinking twice. And there are other times when white fragility is so self-obsessed, so over the top that the damage it inflicts on marginalized people becomes immediately apparent.

For a year I worked for a short-term missions site on the West Side of Chicago. Our program was located in a Black neighborhood and intentionally brought students to learn about all the amazing ways God was already working in Black neighborhoods through Black people. We hosted about fifty people each week of the summer, and smaller

groups through the year. Most of the white participants were a little nervous when they climbed out
of their vans, having never spent time in a predominately Black community. But my staff of college
students would quickly win them over and before
long the groups would be traipsing around the city,
hopping on and off the El like pros as they learned
about our hood.

One group, however, couldn't get over their fears
about the neighborhood—or the fact that Austin,
the director of the program, was not a white man.

I sensed something was wrong as soon as the
group pulled up. Typically, young people would
pour out of the bus, eager to stretch their legs after
being cooped up for the hours-long drive. Their excitement would turn into a flurry of bright colored
bags, blankets, pillows, and matching T-shirts. But
this group was different. They just sat on the bus.
It was almost eerie. After a while, my staff went to
greet them, and somehow managed to coax them
off the bus and into the room where we held the
opening service.

There were worship songs, icebreakers, introduc-
tions, and a tour of the church to get everyone accli-
mated to the new space. Usually this would last for
about an hour, after which I would steal away the

parents for an orientation of their own. But right in the middle of the icebreakers, the youth pastor asked me if she could speak with Austin, the director. When I informed her that I, in fact, was Austin, her eyes grew wide. She looked away from me toward her group, then back at me again, her eyes still bulging. I had a sinking feeling that the shock wouldn't pass with an awkward laugh.

She finally spoke. "Oh." Though she hadn't asked me anything, I responded as if she had. "My name is Austin and I am the director of this program."

She exhaled. "Could the rest of the parents and I have a word with you? It's important."

I nodded and asked one of my staff members to take them to the conference room where I always led the adult orientation. I needed a second. I knew from the woman's reaction that this was going to be awful. It was.

When I walked into the room, all six of the parents gave me the same shocked look. I repeated what was becoming a mantra that evening: "My name is Austin, and I am the director of this program." What came next was an onslaught of questions rooted in their fears of Blackness. They started with a desire to know who was "really" in charge, as if a white person would suddenly make an appearance. Thirty minutes later they ended with questions about the possibility of being killed by Black gang members. The message behind their questions was clear: My neighborhood was untrustworthy, and so was my Black female body.

The end of the parent meeting was usually when I would share about the amazing work happening in our community and hand out the schedule of nonprofits I'd prepared for them to visit. But I didn't trust this group enough to stick to the schedule. I informed them that in light of their clear discomfort, I wanted to make their group a little larger—allowing them to travel as ten to twelve, rather than four to five people. I would need time to talk with the directors of our partner programs and confirm everything.

The parents were so grateful to be able to travel in larger groups, they didn't mind the last-minute change in plans. Little did they know, my first priority was protecting the nonprofits. I refused to allow their toxic ideas and offensive assumptions anywhere near the organizations, the people, I loved. Instead, I arranged to send them to a massive homeless shelter, one with strong religious underpinnings that this group would appreciate. I knew the bulk of their time would be spent on a tour of the facility, leaving very little time for the group to interact with actual folks who were experiencing homelessness. They went on the visit, and many people in the group came back from their trip genuinely moved by the experience. But it wasn't enough to salvage the situation. An hour or so after returning from the shelter—twenty-four hours into a planned weeklong trip—the youth pastor informed me the group was leaving. The parents' fear of a Black neighborhood had won out in the end.

As the youth group packed their things, the mothers ducked into an empty conference room to talk with my staff. With eyes downcast, the mothers began to tearfully confess their fears. They wanted to thank my staff for opening their eyes to their own racism. My staff listened patiently. But just as they started to approach something close to forgiveness, another white parent, a father, entered the room. He immediately took over the discussion. He shared that the first thing he had done when they arrived in front of our building was call the local police department and ask if it was safe for white people to be here. He then noted his disappointment that there was no "welcoming committee" offering them safe passage for the fifteen feet between the bus and the building. As he continued to list his grievances, he started referring to me in the third person as "the director" though I was sitting two feet from him. "You mean Austin?" one of the apologetic parents interrupted. "Who is Austin?" he replied, and then continued to list all the other things "the director" had done wrong.

At that point I'd had enough. "This conversation is over," I said. "It's time for you all to leave."

I was livid. But I also knew this was my job—dealing with white people. How far should I have gone to manage their fears? At what point did the group become not only a nuisance but a detriment to the community I love? What would I have done if they'd stayed? What was my responsibility to my white student employees—to believe in the possibility of the group's transformation, or to give them the reality that not everyone is interested in change? And how did I hold that up against my Black student employees, who had to listen to this racist nonsense? What would my supervisor think? What would the board of directors think? How much would this episode cost the organization?

I was making decisions on the fly, and I did the best I could. But I still wonder if I should have waited even twenty-four hours. The first sixty minutes had been damaging enough.

Thank goodness, that group wasn't the only one we hosted that week. Another one showed up a few days later, completely ready to confront their biases as they volunteered at urban gardens, shelters, group homes, and food pantries. This group was more homogenous than the other, but they came prepared to learn.

At the end of the week, this second group sat down with my staff to process their trip. Five or six of the teenagers had gone to a group home that kept an urban garden to supplement groceries in the house. The youth group spent the day working in the garden, and then learned how to cook the proceeds from teenage boys who lived in the home. As they told me how it went, one girl spoke up. "I had a really good time working alongside the guys, but my biggest lesson came after we left." She then recounted how upon their leaving, some of the guys from the home followed them out the door on their way to work.

The girl's father, who was accompanying the group, asked his daughter to turn around. "What would you think of those guys if you hadn't just spent the afternoon with them?"

It only took her a moment to tell the truth. "I would have looked at their skin color and tattoos, the way they dress and their playfulness and assumed they were gang members." She paused for a moment, then declared, "I realized today that I can be racist."

Though she was the first to say it aloud, many members of the youth group had a similar moment by the end of the week. Their confessions were no burden to me or my staff because they took full ownership of what it meant to face their own racism.

It was a painful week, but it taught me that I cannot control expressions of white fragility. Each group was responsible for their own reaction. One indulged their fragility, the other resisted it.

To stay committed to this work, I have learned to accept the constant experience of entrenchment and transformation. On the bad days, when entrenchment is lashing out, tearing down, pretending you don't have a name, this work feels soul crushing, dehumanizing. But on the good days, you witness transformation, openness, a willingness to change one's worldview. And for a brief moment, I can believe in the possibility that we are still inching toward justice.

7

Nice White People

We were on a working retreat. Earlier that day, the seven of us had left the safety of the diverse city and traveled north to a quieter, whiter town. After working for a couple hours, my group decided to take a break from the hotel conference room. We spent the rest of the morning sailing—we'll get to that in a second, but let's just say it didn't go well for me. After departing the boat, we ended up at a restaurant bar with a distinctly nautical theme for lunch.

We were waiting for our drinks when a co-worker walked over to me. "Are you doing okay?" she asked. I thought she was referring to the reason our sailing trip had ended early. I was not used to being on a boat. Out on the water, my stomach had felt like it was moving around as much as the waves. While everyone conversed and laughed on deck, wearing big sunglasses and leaning against the walls of the boat, I was practicing deep breathing techniques and weighing which would be more embarrassing—throwing up or asking the captain if we could return to shore.

But that's not what she meant. "I noticed you're the only person of color here and I know that can be uncomfortable," she said with great concern.

She meant well, and part of me was really proud of her for noticing. I was pretty sure this was a moment of growth for her to walk into a room and realize it's white. But truth be told, I was equally perplexed by the timing of her question. She was right. I was the only person of color in the bar that day. But I had also been the only person of color on the bus we drove up in, in the conference room we occupied for our work, on the boat we had just disembarked. And when we returned to our workplace, I would often be the only person of color in the room again.

I smiled, thanked her for noticing, and told her I was fine. To point out that I am always aware of my color, even with her and our fellow co-workers, would have been too much for that moment. I would have been telling her that her whiteness is not fundamentally different than the whiteness of the space we currently occupied. It would have threatened her sense of goodness—of being a "good white person," the kind who notices when we are in a restaurant with no people of color. In my experience, white people who believe they are safe often prove dangerous when that identity is challenged.

This is in part because most white people still believe that they are good and the true racists are easy to spot. The true racists wouldn't have hired me, wouldn't have brought me on this trip, wouldn't have noticed the homogenous environment. My colleagues were much too nice to be racists.

I don't know where this belief comes from, but I do know it has consequences. When you believe niceness disproves the presence of racism, it's easy to start believing bigotry is rare, and that the label *racist* should be applied only to mean-spirited, intentional acts of discrimination. The problem with this framework—besides being a gross misunderstanding of how racism operates in systems and structures enabled by nice people—is that it obligates me to be nice in return, rather than truthful. I am expected to come closer to the racists. Be nicer to them. Coddle them.

Even more, if most white people are good, innocent, lovely folks who are just angry or scared or ignorant, it naturally follows that whenever racial tension arises, I must be the problem. I am not kind enough, patient enough, warm enough. I don't have enough understanding for the white heart, white feelings, white needs. It does not matter that I don't always feel like teaching white people through my pain, through the disappointment of allies who gave up and colaborers who left. It does not matter that the "well-intentioned" questions hurt my feelings or that the decisions made in all-white meetings affect me differently than they do everyone else. If my feelings do not fit the narrative of white innocence and goodness, the burden of change gets placed on me.

When this narrative of goodness is disrupted by the unplanned utterance of racial slurs, jokes, rants, or their kind, whiteness has perfected another tool for defending its innocence. I call it the Relational Defense. It happens in the media all the time. A government official, teacher, pastor, or principal is caught on tape saying something that is clearly racist. But rather than confess and seek transformation, the person defends their "goodness" by appealing to the relationships of those who "know" them.

"I am not racist! Just ask [blank]. She knows me."

"My family and friends know my heart. They
will tell you I couldn't be racist."

"I have a Black spouse/child/friend. I don't have
a racist bone in my body."

PR-challenged politicians and celebrities aren't the only ones who use the Relational Defense, and white people are often willing to extend this defense to one another. Once, after inviting me to lead a diversity training session for volunteers at a food pantry, the organization's director explained why she thought the training was necessary. She told me a story about a committed volunteer, a white woman, getting into an altercation with an older Black female shopper. Though I hadn't been there when the argument happened, the details didn't surprise me. The director admitted that the volunteer had treated the shopper like a child, using a condescending, paternalistic tone. It wasn't long before the shopper had had enough. Things escalated from there until the pair were yelling back and forth.

The director then cut to the white volunteer's reaction. "She marched into my office after the shopper left, shouting about how ungrateful the woman was. She said she wanted to go home early because she was afraid the woman would come back with

her gang friends and blow her head off just for trying to help her."

The director summarized, "So you can see, we
do need more diversity training. But the volunteer
isn't racist. I know her—she has Black friends, just
not *poor* Black friends. Her problem, and maybe
other volunteers', too, is their class privilege."

I had only just met this well-meaning director,
so I wasn't sure how to point out the false dichot-
omy. It implied that if a person is nice (as evidenced
by the fact that they have Black friends), then they
couldn't possibly be racist or bigoted. Never mind
that the woman had blatantly employed racial
stereotypes to demean the character of the Black
woman; if the volunteer was nice to rich Black people, it meant she couldn't possibly be racist.

White people desperately want to believe that
only the lonely, isolated "whites only" club members are racist. This is why the word *racist* offends
"nice white people" so deeply. It challenges their
self-identification as good people. Sadly, most white
people are more worried about being called racist
than about whether or not their actions are in fact
racist or harmful.

But the truth is, even the monsters—the Klan
members, the faces in the lynch mob, the murder-

ers who bombed churches—they all had friends and family members. Each one of them was connected to people who would testify that they had good hearts. They had families who loved them, friends who came over for dinner, churches where they made small talk with the pastor after the service. The monster has always been well dressed and well loved.

But I suspect that white people really don't want to believe that we (people of color) know them, too. They want to believe their proximity to people of color makes them immune. That if they smile at people of color, hire a person of color, read books by people of color, marry or adopt a person of color, we won't sense the ugliness of racism buried in the psyche and ingrained in the heart. White people don't want to believe that we sense the discomfort, hear the ignorance, notice the ways they process race, our bodies, our presence. We know them; we know they are racist.

Entertaining a discussion about race with someone who believes in white innocence often feels like entering the twilight zone. This is largely because those who believe in white innocence don't have enough of a knowledge base to participate meaningfully in the discussion. They haven't educated themselves through books or courses. They are unfamiliar with the lexicon on race, not realizing their words have particular meanings. Their understanding of both America's racial history and current racial landscape is lacking. But this does not prevent them from being convinced of their rightness and need to reassert dominance.

White people are notorious for trying to turn race conversations into debates, and then becoming angry or dismissive when people of color won't participate. White people believe this is because people of color haven't thought it through or are stumped by a well-made point. But the truth is, oftentimes people of color don't have the time, energy, or willpower to teach the white person enough to turn the conversation into a real debate. To do so would be a ton of work.

Even on the occasion when a conversation actually proves itself productive, Black folks still have to be on the lookout for white fragility's cousin: white guilt.

I don't have much use for white guilt anymore. I used to interpret white guilt as an early sign of a change in heart, a glimpse that a movie, program, or speaker had broken through and was producing a changed mind. While that may or may not be true, for those on the receiving end, white guilt is like having tar dry all over your hands and heart. It takes so much work to peel off the layers, rub away the stickiness, get rid of the smell. Unsolicited confessions inspired by a sense of guilt are often poured over Black bodies in search of their own relief.

I experienced this self-indulgent desire for relief after a church celebration for MLK Day. During the service, my friend Jenny and I stood on the church stage, recounting the story of our friendship—formed during the Sankofa trip, back in college. We weaved together our personal stories, ending with specific details from the conversation on that bus. She chose images that would play on the screen behind us as we spoke, hoping those in the congregation would feel some sense of sitting on the bus with us, experiencing what we did. We talked about the first time someone called me a nigger, the disrespectful plantation tour, the horror of the lynching museum. It worked. Sort of.

By the time we stepped off the stage, white people were lining up to offer their racist confessions. A man who looked to be in his thirties: "I once called someone the n–word, and I am so ashamed." A white woman in her early twenties: "My parents wouldn't let me date a Black man, and it only just occurred to me." A forty-ish woman who told me she prided herself on spending time with the Black worship leaders of the church but went on to share, "At my workplace, there is an Indian woman who is often discussed behind her back, but I've never stood up for her."

On and on the confessions went, but none was healing to my soul. Clearly the congregation had been moved by our story. They were thinking through their personal histories. But the stories of hate—only minor incidents in the lives of the confessors—reminded me of the ease with which racism is practiced on a daily basis.

After half an hour of this, I checked in with Jenny. "Is anyone making their confessions to you?" I asked.

"No," she replied. "No one." But it turned out I wasn't alone. The most prominent Black female worship leaders on stage that day were hearing confessions left and right, too. Black women were bearing the brunt of these stories as white attenders sought relief from guilt over the ways they had participated in racism. None of them seemed to consider how their confessions affected the people hearing them.

The same happened when I spoke at a conference in South Carolina just a few months after the

Charleston shooting. The room was predominately white, and the murders at Mother Emanuel AME were still very much on the minds of the people gathered.

My talk was really well received. The audience cried and laughed in all the right places. They *amen*ed and *hhhhmmm*ed just when I had hoped they would. But then the confessions began.

For the final two days of the conference, I was treated to stories of racist parents at holiday dinner parties, Confederate flags adorning homes, and passive church pastors who think the answer to racial justice is just being nice to all people. None of these confessions involved me. No one was apologizing for not listening to me, for being mean to me, or judging me unfairly. But after I had heard all of those confessions, it felt personal. It felt like I was sitting at the table when the racist joke was made and the confessor said nothing. It felt like I was in the home with the Confederate flag that bothered no one else but me. It felt that way because for every confessor, my body had become the stand-in for the actual people who had been harmed in those situations. I was left with the weight of these moments I hadn't experienced. I was expected to offer absolution.

But I am not a priest for the white soul.

The more tired I get, the more I have to un-
glue myself from these offensive, painful stories for
which white people expect an absolution I cannot
give. They want me to tell them "it's okay" and give
them a handy excuse for their behavior. Youth, ignorance, innocence—anything to make them feel
better. White people really want this to be what
reconciliation means: a Black person forgiving
them for one racist sin. But just as I cannot make
myself responsible for the transformation of white
people, neither can I offer relief for their souls.

So I don't accept confessions like these anymore. Nowadays, when someone confesses about
their racist uncle or that time they said the n–word,
I determine to offer a challenge toward transformation. For most confessions, this is as simple as
asking, "So what are you going to do differently?"
The question lifts the weight off my shoulders and
forces the person to move forward, resisting the
easy comfort of having spoken the confession. The
person could, of course, dissolve into excuses, but
at that point the weight of that decision belongs to
them, not to me.

I once received a heartfelt apology from a conference planner who felt bad for making purposeful
decisions that uplifted white women above women

of color as presenters. She explained her thinking at that time, spoke a little about her reflection on the moment, and shared vulnerably about the difficulties of being a conference planner. I was intrigued—not by the confession itself but by the potential that her change of heart could lead to changes in the conferences she oversaw.

And so, rather than accept her apology and close my computer, I asked her to think about how those decisions could be prevented in the future. I offered a couple suggestions: "Perhaps in the future, people of color could receive the most airtime during the conference. Or perhaps you could make a powerful statement by making people of color the highest-paid presenters—a nod to their value, expertise, and the emotional labor of discussing race and justice." I don't know if anything I suggested will go beyond that email. But I enjoyed the imaginative process of making suggestions to someone who professed a desire to change. Whether or not anything I proposed manifested itself was not my responsibility—not my weight to carry. She could decide the significance of her own confession and determine what it would take to fulfill her own reflection on the moment. That was work I was happy to leave between her and the Holy Spirit.

8

The Story We Tell

Not long ago, I was sitting in a diversity training for a new job. Our group slumped into folding chairs beneath the almost blue fluorescent lights. We were halfway through the three-day workshop, doing an activity that left the white women in our group rather emotional. Our facilitators tried to coax our group into discussion, but after giving them short and to-the-point answers, we descended into the kind of silence workshop facilitators hate—the silence that feels so warm and comfortable, it could last forever. And then it came.

Our collective silence was shattered by a trembling white female voice: "I just can't believe it. This is so much to take in. I mean, I had no idea." Inhale. "This is just unbelievable. Why didn't anyone teach us this? I feel so cheated, deceived. I mean, really." Inhale. "This is going to sound crazy. I know it sounds crazy, but I really didn't know that slavery happened on purpose. Like on purpose." Inhale. "I don't know. I just kinda thought that it just . . . happened." Inhale. Her sobbing then filled the room as she grappled for the first time with our country's real history.

Slavery was no accident.

We didn't trip and fall into black subjugation.

Racism wasn't a bad joke that just never went away.

It was all on purpose.

Every bit of it was on purpose.

Racial injustices, like slavery and our system of mass incarceration, were purposeful inventions, but instead of seeking to understand how we got here, the national narrative remains filled with comforting myths, patchwork time lines, and colonial ideals. Like the sobbing woman in the workshop, many Americans try to live comfortably in ignorance of America's racial history.

We have not thoroughly assessed the bodies snatched from dirt and sand to be chained in a cell. We have not reckoned with the horrendous, violent mass kidnapping that we call the Middle Passage.

We have not been honest about all of America's complicity—about the wealth the South earned on the backs of the enslaved, or the wealth the North gained through the production of enslaved hands. We have not fully understood the status symbol that owning bodies offered. We have not confronted the humanity, the emotions, the heartbeats of the multiple generations who were born into slavery and died in it, who never tasted freedom on America's land.

The same goes for the Civil War. We have refused to honestly confront the fact that so many were willing to die in order to hold the freedom of others in their hands. We have refused to acknowledge slavery's role at all, preferring to boil things down to the far more palatable "states' rights." We have not confessed that the end of slavery was so bitterly resented, the rise of Jim Crow became inevitable—and with it, a belief in Black inferiority that lives on in hearts and minds today.

We have painted the hundred-year history of Jim Crow as little more than mean signage and the inconvenience that white people and Black people could not drink from the same fountain. But those signs weren't just "mean." They were perpetual reminders of the swift humiliation and brutal violence that could be suffered at any moment in the presence of whiteness. Jim Crow meant paying taxes for services one could not fully enjoy; working for meager wages; and owning nothing that couldn't be snatched away. For many black families, it meant never building wealth and never having legal recourse for injustice. The mob violence, the burned-down homes, the bombed churches and businesses, the Black bodies that were lynched every couple of days—Jim Crow was walking through life measuring every step.

Even our celebrations of the Civil Rights Movement are sanitized, its victories accentuated while the battles are whitewashed. We have not come to grips with the spitting and shouting, the pulling and tugging, the clubs, dogs, bombs, and guns, the passion and vitriol with which the rights of Black Americans were fought against. We have not acknowledged the bloodshed that often preceded victory. We would rather focus on the beautiful words of Martin Luther King Jr. than on the terror he and protestors endured at marches, boycotts, and from behind jail doors. We don't want to acknowledge that for decades, whiteness fought against every civil right Black Americans sought—from sitting at lunch counters and in integrated classrooms to the right to vote and have a say in how our country was run.

We like to pretend that all those white faces who carried protest signs and batons, who turned on their sprinklers and their fire hoses, who wrote against the demonstrations and preached against the changes, just disappeared. We like to pretend that they were won over, transformed, the moment King proclaimed, "I have a dream." We don't want to acknowledge that just as Black people who experienced Jim Crow are still alive, so are the white people who vehemently protected it—who drew red lines around Black neighborhoods and divested them of support given to average white citizens. We ignore that white people still avoid Black neighborhoods, still don't want their kids going to predominantly Black schools, still don't want to destroy segregation.

The moment Black Americans achieved freedom from enslavement, America could have put to death the idea of Black inferiority. But whiteness was not prepared to sober up from the drunkenness of power over another people group. Whiteness was not ready to give up the ability to control, humiliate, or do violence to any Black body in the vicinity—all without consequence.

Ultimately, the reason we have not yet told the truth about this history of Black and white America is that telling an ordered history of this nation would mean finally naming America's commitment to violent, abusive, exploitative, immoral white supremacy, which seeks the absolute control of Black bodies. It would mean doing something about it.

How long will it be before we finally choose to connect all the dots? How long before we confess the history of racism embedded in our systems of housing, education, health, criminal justice, and more? How long before we dig to the root?

Because it is the truth that will set us free.

Sadly, too many of us in the church don't live like we believe this. We live as if we are afraid acknowledging the past will tighten the chains of injustice rather than break them. We live as if the ghosts of the past will snatch us if we walk through the valley of the shadow of death. So instead we walk around the valley, talk around the valley. We speak of the valley with cute euphemisms:

> "We just have so many divisions in this country."
> "If we could just get better at diversity, we'd be
>   so much better off."
> "We are experiencing some cultural changes."

Our only chance at dismantling racial injustice is being more curious about its origins than we are worried about our comfort. It's not a comfortable conversation for any of us. It is risky and messy. It is haunting work to recall the sins of our past. But is this not the work we have been called to anyway? Is this not the work of the Holy Spirit to illuminate truth and inspire transformation?

It's haunting. But it's also holy.

And when we talk about race today, with all the pain packed into that conversation, the Holy Spirit remains in the room. This doesn't mean the conversations aren't painful, aren't personal, aren't charged with emotion. But it does mean we can survive. We can survive honest discussions about slavery, about convict leasing, about stolen land, deportation, discrimination, and exclusion. We can identify the harmful politics of gerrymandering, voter suppression, criminal justice laws, and policies that disproportionately affect people of color negatively. And we can expose the actions of white institutions—the history of segregation and white flight, the real impact of all-white leadership, the racial disparity in wages, and opportunities for advancement. We can lament and mourn. We can be livid and enraged. We can be honest. We can tell the truth. We can trust that the Holy Spirit is here. We must.

For only by being truthful about how we got here can we begin to imagine another way.

9

Creative Anger

In 1961 James Baldwin, perhaps the greatest American essayist of the twentieth century, stated the following in a recorded panel discussion:

> To be a Negro in this country and to be relatively conscious, is to be in a rage almost all the time. So that the first problem is how to control that rage so that it won't destroy you. Part of the rage is this: it isn't only what is happening to you, but it's what's happening all around you all of the time, in the face of the most extraordinary and criminal indifference, the indifference and ignorance of most white people in this country.

Baldwin wasn't lying. I have become very intimate with anger.

It is rage inducing to be told that we can do anything we put our minds to, when we work at companies and ministries where no one above middle management looks like us. It is rage inducing to know my body is being judged differently at every turn—when I am late to work, when I choose to eat lunch alone, when I am expressing hurt or anger. I become either a stand-in for another Black female body—without distinction between our size, our hair, our color, our voices, our interests, our names, our personalities—or a stand-in for the worst stereotypes—sassy, disrespectful, uncontrollable, or childlike and in need of whiteness to protect me from my [Black] self.

These indignities follow us home, too, when we open the newspaper or turn on the TV. Gross references to Serena Williams's body as animal-like. The reinforcement of Black inferiority as when *The New York Times* publishes a piece saying Viola Davis is not "classically beautiful." The media often seem gleeful when given the opportunity to tear down Black women, and if not careful, these attacks can chip away at our self-esteem. But words are hardly the worst of it. If we look at statistics and standards of living, we find a host of racial disparities that have persisted over decades—wages, home ownership, job accessibility, health care, treatment by law enforcement, and the list goes on. For us, these aren't just statistics—they are the facts of life for us and our mothers, our sisters, our friends and neighbors.

Meanwhile, whiteness twiddles its thumbs with feigned innocence and shallow apologies. Diversity gets treated like a passing trend, a friendly group project in which everyone takes on equal risks and rewards. In the mind of whiteness, half-baked efforts at diversity are enough, because the status quo is fine. It is better than slavery, better than Jim Crow. What more could Black people possibly ask than this—to not be overtly subject to the white will? "Is there more?" white innocence asks before bursting into tears at the possibility that we would dare question its sincerity.

It's hard to be calm in a world made for whiteness.

I've met a number of white people who adamantly resist thinking of themselves as a community, but I cannot imagine resisting my identity as a member of the Black community. I feel kinship and responsibility, pride, belonging, and connection with people simply because of a shared racial and cultural background.

When I pass a Black person being pulled over by the police, I wonder if they are innocent. I wonder how often this happens to them, and I wonder if they need help. Even in my childhood years, when I thought police officers pulled over only guilty people, I would think, *Shoot! Why does the Black person have to get pulled over?* I am not proud of this, but it speaks to how even when the feeling was shame, I still felt connected to random people I didn't know and would never meet, simply because of Blackness.

> When we win the award, I feel something.
> When we get the promotion, I feel something.
> When we break barriers, I feel something.

But I also feel something when we are dying in the streets. When we are derided for our bodies even as white women try to imitate them. When feminism is limited to the needs of whiteness, or when Blackness is used for profit without acknowledging the brilliance of the creators.

I feel something when a white woman mocks the body of Serena Williams by stuffing padding in her skirt and top. When First Lady Michelle Obama is called a monkey. When nine men and women are murdered in a church because they are Black.

I feel anger.

Even more frustrating, there are so few acceptable occasions for my rage to be expressed. Because I am a Black person, my anger is considered dangerous, explosive, and unwarranted. Because I am a woman, my anger supposedly reveals an emotional problem or gets dismissed as a temporary state that will go away once I choose to be rational. Because I am a Christian, my anger is dismissed as a character flaw, showing just how far I have turned from Jesus. Real Christians are nice, kind, forgiving—and anger is none of those things.

Though I knew these interpretations to be ludicrous, dealing with these reactions to any hint of my anger was enough to prevent me from speaking it. The boldness I possessed in school melted away in the face of supervisors, performance reviews, benefits packages, and the backlash that came from expecting more out of my Church.

In moments when I was angry, I used to wish I was *that* Black girl. You know the one. The one who snaps her gum. Who claps out every word when angry. The one who rolls her eyes and you feel it in your bones. The one who always says what she thinks—who begins her sentences with "First of all . . ." and then lists what you ain't gon do. I wanted to be the Black girl who white people are afraid of making angry.

But that Black girl wasn't me. I longed for the immediate release of rage, but my mild-mannered nature would not allow me this luxury.

I wished I was Zora Neale Hurston, genuinely confused by any white people who would deny themselves her company. I wanted to be Nina Simone, quick to check anyone who would underestimate the beauty of her Blackness. I wanted to be Angela Davis, intellectual and bold, speaking truth to power about society's treatment of Black people.

I wanted to be anyone but mild-mannered me.

And so my anger would boil, below the surface. I was launched right back into Dunbar's poem. *Austin wears the mask that grins and lies.*

Instead of anger, I would try to communicate other emotions that I thought might receive an audience—pain, disappointment, sadness. I would roll up my sleeves and reveal the scars, cut myself open and hope the blood that emerged would move my listeners. I believed that I was taking Baldwin's advice, that I was working to not be destroyed by my own rage. I thought I was getting to the bottom of it, but really I was denying it, covering it. All those years ago, on a bus in the South, I had watched a young Black woman state her rage with clarity and calm, despite how anyone else on that bus felt. But I couldn't do it. I was more afraid of my own rage than I realized.

I tried to be the wise, patient teacher, the composed one. I tried to wear an air of unbotheredness, standing on something akin to moral superiority. But ultimately, these were attempts at self-restriction. I left my humanity at the door.

Then Audre Lorde saved me. In her book *Sister Outsider,* Lorde wrote an essay entitled "The Uses of Anger." She writes that anger is not a shortcoming to be denied, but a creative force that tells us when something is wrong.

> Every woman has a well-stocked arsenal of anger potentially useful against those oppressions, personal and institutional, which brought that anger into being. Focused with precision it can become a powerful source of energy serving progress and change ... Anger expressed and translated into action in the service of our vision and our future is a liberating and strengthening act of clarification.

A sense of freedom fell over me as I read her words. Anger is not inherently destructive. My anger can be a force for good. My anger can be creative and imaginative, seeing a better world that doesn't yet exist. It can fuel a righteous movement toward justice and freedom. I don't need to fear my own anger. I don't have to be afraid of myself. I am not mild-mannered. I am passionate and strong and clear-eyed and focused on continuing the legacy of proclaiming the human dignity of Black bodies.

Once upon a time I was mad that I wasn't *that* Black girl. But I am not her. I am not the gum-snapping, head-rolling, don't-think-I-won't-make-a-scene Black girl. So who am I? That is the question I had to ask in order to make use of my anger.

I am not Zora, but I can decide not to measure my effectiveness in the ebbs and flows of white affirmation. I am not Nina, but I can defend Black dignity through writing and preaching. I am not Angela, but I am learning to speak truth to power in ways that are equally invitational and challenging.

It was hard at first, trusting my voice of anger. But Black life is full of opportunities to practice. And so I did. I wrote. And I spoke. And I engaged with others, and then I wrote some more. Just like Lorde promised, my anger led to creativity, to connections with others who were angry, too. My anger didn't destroy me. It did not leave me alone and desolate. On the contrary, my anger undergirded my calling, my vocation. It gave me the courage to say hard things and to write like Black lives are on the line.

It shouldn't have surprised me. I serve a God who experienced and expressed anger. One of the most meaningful passages of Scripture for me is found in the New Testament, where Jesus leads a one-man protest inside the Temple walls. Jesus shouts at the corrupt Temple officials, overturns furniture, sets animals free, blocks the doorways with his body, and carries a weapon—a whip—through the place. Jesus throws folks out the building, and in so doing creates space for the most marginalized to come in: the poor, the wounded, the children. I imagine the next day's newspapers called Jesus's anger destructive. But I think those without power would've said that his anger led to freedom—the freedom of belonging, the freedom of healing, and the freedom of participating as full members in God's house.

Interlude:

How to Survive Racism in an Organization That Claims to Be Antiracist

10. Ask why they want you. Get as much clarity as possible on what the organization has read about you, what they understand about you, what they assume are your gifts and strengths. What does the organization hope you will bring to the table? Do those answers align with your reasons for wanting to be at the table?

9. Define your terms. You and the organization may have different definitions of words like *justice, diversity,* or *antiracism.* Ask for definitions, examples, or success stories to give you a better idea of how the organization understands and embodies these words. Also ask

about who is in charge and who is held accountable for these efforts. Then ask yourself if you can work within that structure.

8. Hold the organization to the highest vision they committed to for as long as you can. Be ready to move if the leaders aren't prepared to pursue their own stated vision.

7. Find your people. If you are going to push back against the system or push leadership forward, it's wise not to do so alone. Build or join an antiracist cohort within the organization.

6. Have mentors and counselors on standby. Don't just choose a really good friend or a parent when seeking advice. It's important to have one or two mentors who can give advice based on their personal knowledge of the organization and its leaders. You want someone who can help you navigate the particular politics of your organization.

5. Practice self-care. Remember that you are a whole person, not a mule to carry the racial sins of the organization. Fall in love, take your children to the park, don't miss doctors' visits,

read for pleasure, dance with abandon, have lots of good sex, be gentle with yourself.

4. Find donors who will contribute to the cause. Who's willing to keep the class funded, the diversity positions going, the social justice center operating? It's important for the organization to know the members of your cohort aren't the only ones who care. Demonstrate that there are stakeholders, congregation members, and donors who want to see real change.

3. Know your rights. There are some racist things that are just mean, but others are against the law. Know the difference, and keep records of it all.

2. Speak. Of course, context matters. You must be strategic about when, how, to whom, and about which situations you decide to call out. But speak. Find your voice and use it.

1. Remember: You are a creative being who is capable of making change. But it is not your responsibility to transform an entire organization.

10

The Ritual of Fear

A lot of people know the names Trayvon Martin, Eric Garner, and Michael Brown, thanks to the three Black women who coined the phrase Black Lives Matter and launched a justice movement to address the needs of Black America. But for me, personally, there was another precipitating event. One life that forced me to ask the question *Do all Black lives matter?*

My cousin Dalin was a big guy. He stood about six feet tall, with a muscular frame that gave him the illusion of having another two to three inches in height. He always dressed his best—bright-colored, oversize shirts and designer jeans made for Black men. His shoes were what we would have called crispy back when we were kids. I sometimes wondered if he kept shoe cleaner in his back pocket.

More than his style, though, Dalin was known for his laugh. If Dalin was six feet tall, his laugh was twelve. He had a short chuckle for when things amused him, but if he really thought something was funny, you'd hear him around the block. It was a deep, bellowing laugh that sounded too old for his young body—more like the laugh possessed by grandfathers who've lived a thousand lives and need to invite the whole neighborhood into their joy.

Like many Black men, Dalin was funny as hell. At family gatherings, where he had more competition for the center of attention, he usually stayed pretty quiet. Or so you thought, until you sat next to him and heard his side comments and sarcasm. Dalin knew the quirks of every person in our family, and his loving, easy quips contained too much truth to not elicit a laugh.

Despite being my first cousin, Dalin always seemed just a little out of reach. He was a boy, and I was a girl. He was a cool and confident sixteen when I was still a self-conscious and shy eight-year-old. His family lived in Akron, and mine in Toledo. We moved around each other in concentric circles, only occasionally occupying the same space.

One year during Christmas break, my aunts and uncles, cousins and friends, had crammed into the warm, creaky house in Akron where my father was raised. While the adults gathered in the kitchen, I snuck upstairs to my grandmother's room, where she lay in bed under warm blankets, watching her twenty-inch tube television with the squiggly lines and long antenna. I was eight years old and didn't often get my grandmother to myself, so I happily sat on the floor, talking about the commercials and laughing at the silly characters on the screen.

All of a sudden, a commotion downstairs broke the calm. The front door slammed—*bang!*—and Dalin's voice shot through the floor, more high-pitched than usual and frantic in sound. His mother's voice responded, matching in cadence but three octaves higher. "What? Oh, no you're not!" she started to say before Dalin cut her off. The noise grew steadily. My grandmother and I only caught snatches of words and phrases, but the one that stood out was the word *gun*. My grandmother and I looked at each other with eyebrows raised. She didn't move, so I didn't either.

The yelling stopped as footsteps pounded on the stairs, heading up toward us. I could tell my grandmother knew it was Dalin. She turned toward the door before he reached it. "What's going on?" she asked as he came into view.

My cool cousin had disappeared. This teenager, lit only by the glow from the small TV, was shook. "I was out with my friends when some dude took my shoes," Dalin said, cracking his knuckles.

My grandmother's confusion mirrored my own. "Took your shoes?" she asked.

Dalin explained that he had just bought a new pair of sneakers. After leaving the store, he and his friends were held up at gunpoint. His crew didn't carry weapons, so Dalin had no choice but to hand the bright white shoes over. And he was pissed.

"So what are you going to do now?" our grandmother asked, clearly looking for an honest answer. Dalin didn't hesitate. "I'm looking for a gun to go get my shoes back." His knuckles cracked again.

My grandmother and I stared at him in horror. I wonder if her mind was doing what mine was. I was so afraid he would go outside and never come home—but even at a young age, I knew this wasn't about his shoes. This was about his pride. Not the icky, arrogant kind. I mean the pride inherent in being human. The kind that flares when a stranger believes your life is worth less than a pair of shoes. I could hear the desire not quite for revenge but for the righting of a wrong. A desire to rearrange the world and go back to being in control, being safe, being in charge of what happened that night. And since Dalin was a teenager who'd just paid a lot of money for those tennis shoes . . . I'm thinking he also wanted the shoes back.

I can still see his face, a troubling mix of anger and sadness. I'm not sure it even registered for him that I was there. But that was the moment when I understood the rules governing my cousin's life were different than those governing my own. I knew going to the police wasn't a viable option for him. But if the same had happened to me, not only was I unaware of where I could possibly get a gun in my world but I wouldn't even have known who to ask. Dalin lived in a world I knew only through headlines. So I believed him. I believed his description of his world, and I was afraid for him. I wanted him to live.

It's a fear I came to know well as I got older. Fear that my father won't make it home when he travels through white rural Ohio for work, or that my brother's deep intellect won't stop someone from assuming he's a criminal. It's the fear that my husband will be mistaken for someone else, or that I won't be able to protect my little boy when my womb no longer hides him. Fear that my own body will be violated by the state.

Sometimes the fear is debilitating. As I write this, my husband has left to visit his parents. He must drive two hours across the state of Michigan to get there and two hours back. I am actively trying not to imagine him being pulled over, frisked. I am actively trying not to imagine his anger rising, his tongue getting the best of him. I am actively trying not to imagine. I don't want to pass my anxiety to him.

So when he left this morning, I gave him a hug. I told him to be safe. I said, "Promise you will come back to me," and he knew I was not joking.

He looked me in the eyes. "I will be fine. I'll call you when I get there." I nodded and smiled and pretended to feel better.

Sometimes when I'm hanging out with my white friends, they notice that I call my husband, Tommie, whenever I arrive, and then call him again when I'm leaving. They've never teased me outright for this, but I have seen the looks of amusement pass between them. I know they think Tommie and I do this because we are inseparable, or because he is demanding. For a moment my feminist card is revoked in their eyes. But these are our rituals for staying safe when we're out in the world. This is how we beat back the fear.

I first felt it with Dalin. And even though he didn't go back into the night thanks to our uncles' intervention, I have felt that fear ever since. So have countless other Black parents, Black siblings, Black couples, Black communities. We fear the overreactions of white people who clutch their purses in elevators and lock their doors when we walk by. We fear the overreaction of police who assume they are in danger when they have the wrong suspect or when we are unarmed. We fear that appearing guilty means incurring the repercussions of being guilty. We fear that any public imperfection of our children will lead to extrajudicial, deadly consequences. Even when our babies aren't perfect, even when they are rude or disrespectful, even when they make mistakes or fail, even when their sixteen-year-old brains tell them to do risky, stupid things, we still want them to live. We want them to make it to another day.

But until then, we find ourselves repeating this all-too-familiar ritual of fear.

11

A God for the Accused

After college, I moved to Michigan and enrolled in a master's program for social justice while working full-time. Toward the end of the program, we were required to read *A Place to Stand*, Jimmy Santiago Baca's bracing memoir of life in prison. That book knocked the wind out of me. I had heard stories about innocent men going away and their harrowing experiences of life behind bars. But even though Baca did in fact commit the crime that sent him to prison, I couldn't stomach the life he described. As I read about the violence, the abuse, the pressure of always being ready to defend oneself, all I could think about was Dalin.

Dalin and I never became close over the years. He was pursuing a rap career, and studio time required a lot of money, so in order to fund his passion, he sold drugs. It was a bad time to start that kind of a career. Around the time my cousin was emerging from teenager to adult, President Clinton signed an act that called for mandatory minimums for multiple drug offenses, and police departments around the country started cracking down on nonviolent crime. In Black neighborhoods, it was impossible to be a young man of Dalin's build and not get pulled over by the police on a regular basis. He was strip-searched in the streets. He was assaulted by officers who enjoyed his humiliation. And he was arrested . . . a lot.

When I came back to town for the holidays, it was not uncommon to hear Dalin was behind bars. But in years when he could join in the festivities, he was a doting father, thoroughly enjoying the spunky antics of his daughter, who was just learning to walk and talk. When Dalin was home, nothing else mattered—we bowed our heads and thanked God that we had one another.

When I heard Dalin received his third strike, I wasn't sure how to take the news. This wouldn't be just a short stint. This meant a mandatory ten years away from us—the equivalent of my entire high school and college career plus two more years of adulthood. How could anyone process spending that much time in prison for a nonviolent offense?

By the time I enrolled in my master's program and read *A Place to Stand,* Dalin had already been away for a few years. As I turned the pages filled with solitary confinement, violence, and hallucinations, I kept asking myself: *Is this what Dalin is experiencing? Is my cousin learning these rules, fighting to survive the politics of prison? Does he spend his days trying to avoid violence from fellow inmates or guards? Does the staff keep his mail from him as punishment? What is happening to him? Is this what it's like for everyone inside?*

I hadn't reached out to Dalin since he went to prison. I wondered about him, but I wasn't sure how to ask about his incarceration. I knew my cousin's crime wasn't violent, but I didn't know if we were going to talk about it. Could I ask my aunt how he was doing? Did people visit him? Was this a family secret, or was it okay to talk about openly? Every now and then I got up the courage to ask my father about Dalin, but the answers were usually short. I let the subject drop. I think my father knew more than he was telling me.

After reading *A Place to Stand,* though, I decided I wasn't waiting anymore. I would reach out

and try to start a relationship with Dalin. I wasn't
going to wait for his release, or keep my childhood
hope that one day life would bring us together. I
would step into the chasm between us and hope he
would join me there.

I researched how to send a letter to someone in
prison, and then wrote it painstakingly. My handwriting has never looked better. I told Dalin about
life since the last time I had seen him. I was married now and living in Michigan. As a hobby, I had
started researching our family history, so I told him
the things I had discovered about our grandparents
and great-grandparents. How our great-grandfather
was missing a big toe; how even though he could
have passed as white during the war—with light
skin and blue eyes—his draft card listed him as
"colored." I told Dalin I was thinking about him,
but I didn't include the words *I love you*. I was afraid
he would laugh. I knew I deserved it.

Even as I sealed the envelope, I wondered if the
note would reach him. Then I wondered if he'd
bother to respond, since I hadn't talked to him in
years. I didn't know, but I had to try. I put it in the
mail and waited. I waited so long, I almost missed
his reply.

Weeks later, the post office clerk set the letter

on the counter between us. My hands trembled as I picked it up and walked to my car. What if he was offended and just wrote a one-word response? What if the letter was just a monologue handing me my ass for not writing a long time ago? My eyes watered as I read the first line. "Yo, Cuz. Yeah I was surprised to get your letter, but we family so its all love." And then, having absolved me, he went on to respond to everything in my letter, concluding with details about his life inside and hopes for his future after his release. Turned out he already knew about our great-grandfather's missing big toe. Apparently he'd asked about it when he was a little boy, but no one had ever satisfied his curiosity. I smiled, imagining tiny Dalin boldly asking about this missing body part and being completely dismissed by the adults. That sounded accurate, but also like an era that was long gone.

I don't think I've ever felt more overwhelmed by another person offering me mercy and love. I was so excited. I would finally get to know my cousin. I sat down and immediately started the next letter.

I don't know if he ever got it. He died in prison just a few weeks later.

It took hours of calling the prison officials through tears before they told my family what happened. Dalin and some of his friends had been in the yard one day when rain and thunder broke out above them. The men were residing in an honor program, in a separate part of the facility. Though the general population had received the warning about the impending storm, those living in the honor program had not. As the storm grew worse, turning into heavy rain, the men tried to come back inside, but it was too late. Lightning struck and Dalin was gone.

A few days later, we sat waiting for Dalin's wake to officially begin. Pictures from his childhood scrolled across large screens, and I placed my hand on my Bible with his letter tucked into the front. To this day, it is a constant reminder of who my cousin really was—funny, merciful, hopeful, connected to our family history, and wanting to come home. I glanced at his handwriting and cried.

Seven days later, I was standing in church when the anger hit me. The pastor was "opening the doors of the church"—the moment in a service when the minster invites people to become members of the church or recommit their lives to Christ. The Sunday after Dalin died, a young man, about thirty years old, came down front. He spoke with a minister for a couple minutes, then, as was customary, the pastor shared a little bit with the congregation. The young man had just been released from prison. He'd learned about Christ while inside but wanted to make another commitment to God as he started his life again. The church roared in approval, and the man's ten-year-old daughter raced down to the front and into his arms. It was so beautiful. And it pissed me off.

I didn't understand why Dalin hadn't gotten another chance. Just days earlier I'd watched my aunt tell her granddaughter that her father had died, that he was never coming back home. She would never race into her father's arms again.

As the rest of the congregation rose to its feet, praising God and encouraging the family, my legs started to give way. Fury flooded my body. All I could do was lean into the wooden pew and cry. *God, why did you take him?* Who else was I going to blame? My cousin hadn't been killed in a fight; he was struck by lightning, and I believed in a God who controls nature. A God who could have saved his life. What the hell?

My anger didn't scare me. The Bible is filled with stories of God handling anger from people far more important than me. I needed to let someone have it. God was there.

But when I was done fuming at God, having cycled through my grief, I still had some questions: What was the state's responsibility to those who are incarcerated? How many unjust interactions with police had Dalin experienced? How did I feel about laws like mandatory minimums? The questions kept piling up. As I began to study the criminal justice system in relationship to the Black community, I was forced to ask one more question: What did my theology have to say about Black lives that don't look like mine?

Dalin's death challenged me to expand my understanding for racial justice. I could talk all day long about the injustices within the Church, but I needed to be able to speak to the realities of Black life beyond my own privileged experiences—my private white Christian education and ministry life. Most of all, I had to reject the notion that my cousin's life was somehow less valuable because he did not meet the "Christian criteria" of innocence and perfection.

Even as I write these words, I am bracing myself for the reaction of those who will not care, those who will tell me that Dalin's death is his own fault. They will spit out the words *drug dealer,* just as they spit out the word *criminal.* Maybe they'll call him a thug, a nigger, or tell me that the world is better without him in it. But the one word that will go unspoken is the word *black*. Underneath all the other hurtful words, this is the one that whiteness really wants to spew.

Whiteness has never needed much of an excuse for our deaths.

Accused of looking at a white woman. Resisted arrest. Scared the officer. Thought he had a weapon. Had a criminal record (that the officer knew nothing about). Looked suspicious. Looked like someone else.

It doesn't really matter. At the end of the day, Blackness is always the true offense. Whiteness needs just a hint of a reason to maintain its own goodness, assuring itself that there's no reason to worry, because the victim had it coming. He was a drug dealer. A criminal. A thug.

We don't talk about white drug dealers this way. We don't even talk about white *murderers* this way. Somehow, we manage to think of them as people first, who just happened to do something bad. But the same respect is rarely afforded to Black folks. We must always earn the right to live. Perfection is demanded of Blackness before mercy or grace or justice can even be considered. I refuse to live this way.

All those years ago, I learned in church that Jesus understood the poor. Because of Dalin, I realized that Jesus also understood the accused, the incarcerated, the criminals. Jesus was accused. Jesus was incarcerated. Jesus hung on a cross with his crime listed above his crown of thorns. It doesn't bring Dalin back. But it matters to me that my God knows what Dalin's body endured. Suddenly racial justice and reconciliation wasn't limited to Black and white church members; it became a living framework for understanding God's work in the world.

12

We're Still Here

For millions of people—white and Black—the election of Barack Obama was a sign that America had become a postracial society. Even in those early years of optimism, I knew better than to expect so much. I do not want to dismiss the deep meaning I felt watching the Obama family wave at the crowds in Chicago after his victory speech, a feat I myself had called an impossibility just a year before. And yet, beneath the celebration, most of us (Black people) were still afraid. Given America's history of murdering Black civil rights leaders, in our bones we worried that someone would assassinate him for this accomplishment of winning the White House. We were aware of the protests not about his policies but about his race. We saw the signs and the nooses, the comic strips and the billboards, the essays and the articles, the constant condescending language that President Barack Obama simply *"didn't understand"* an issue, a policy, a law, or America itself.

Though it bothered me to no end, I had braced myself for the backlash to Obama's race, at least on the part of average white citizens. The stupid signs, the offensive comics . . . In my mind these were to be expected. The election of Barack Obama had not suddenly ushered in a postracial America. And yet.

What I didn't see coming was Ferguson. Like that moment in the lynching museum years earlier, the gap between history and present closed once again, this time on my living room TV.

It took a while for the mainstream media to realize news was being made in this suburb of St. Louis, but the residents of Ferguson knew. Days later, once cable news caught up, the images began appearing on our television screens nightly. Police faced Black residents as if ready for war. They donned riot gear, held dogs by the leash, threw tear gas, and confronted residents with tanks in front of the damn McDonald's. If all you could see were the police officers, you would've thought these images were from another country, or that the police were staring down folks armed with rifles and bulletproof vests. But in the widened camera lenses, we saw that the standoff was with our parents, our aunts and uncles, our cousins and children. All of them dressed in shorts and T-shirts demanding that an officer be held accountable for the shooting of an unarmed teen.

The parallels to the photos from my history book could not be ignored.

By the time the era called Black Lives Matter began, I was already familiar with the theory that racism never went away; it just evolved. But as I stared at my screen in horror and sadness, watching Black residents being treated like enemies of the state, it seemed to me that racism hadn't evolved at all. Instead of confronting Black residents on horseback with nightsticks, police now showed up in tanks with automatic rifles strapped to their backs.

I was frustrated and sad—and yet it all seemed so familiar. Like I had been here before. Like my parents had been here before. Like my grandparents had been here before.

White people often want me to be grateful for America's so-called racial progress. When I lead trainings, discussing America's history, they want me to praise America for "how far we have come." This is where they want me to place my hope—in the narrative that says things are getting better.

But I cannot.

Don't get me wrong. I am eternally grateful to my ancestors who carried the unbearable weight of slavery. I am grateful for those who lived and loved and worked and played before there was any talk of a national movement to secure equal civil rights. I am grateful for my great-great-great-grandfather, who escaped slavery to join the Union army. For my great-great-grandmother, who refused to ride in the back of the train when traveling to visit her sister in Arkansas. I am grateful for my ancestors' struggle and their survival. But I am not impressed with America's progress.

I am not impressed that slavery was abolished or that Jim Crow ended. I feel no need to pat America on its back for these "achievements." This is how it always should have been. Many call it progress, but I do not consider it praiseworthy that only within the last generation did America reach the baseline for human decency. As comedian Chris Rock says, I suppose these things were progress for white people, but damn. I hope there is progress I can sincerely applaud on the horizon.

Because the extrajudicial killing of Black people is still too familiar.

Because the racist rhetoric that Black people are lazier, more criminal, more undeserving than white people is still too familiar.

Because the locking up of a disproportionate number of Black bodies is still too familiar.

Because the beating of Black people in the streets is still too familiar.

History is collapsing on itself once again.

On Sunday, September 15, 1963, a bomb tore through the walls of the Sixteenth Street Baptist Church in Birmingham, Alabama. Inside, Black congregation members had been preparing for their Sunday service, unaware that members of the Ku Klux Klan had laid sticks of dynamite under the church's stairs. Twenty-two people were injured in the planned attack, and four little girls were killed: Cynthia Wesley, Carole Robertson, and Addie Mae Collins—all fourteen years old—and eleven-year-old Denise McNair.

Just two weeks earlier, Martin Luther King Jr. stood on the steps of the National Mall and gave his famous "I Have a Dream" speech. In the following days, Alabama began integrating high schools and elementary schools for the first time in its history.

The world was changing, and segregationists who worshipped at the altar of white supremacy could not contain their hatred and frustration. This was the third bombing in just eleven days since the integration order—but the first to prove deadly. White folks were making clear that they would rather see Black people die violent deaths than attend school with their children.

Though I grew up hearing this story about the Four Little Girls, there was a lot I didn't know. I didn't know that bombings had been a regular form of intimidation, or that the famous March on Washington had taken place only eighteen days before. What I knew was this: White people had been willing to bomb a Black church, right in the middle of Sunday school, and kill four Black girls. These weren't just words in a history book. I was a teenager who loved being in church. What if I had been born in another day and time?

I stopped wondering when the distance between past and present closed yet again one evening in June 2015, when a white supremacist walked into Emanuel African Methodist Episcopal Church and took as many lives as he could with a Glock 41 handgun. I was just about to turn over and go to sleep when I saw a tweet from an MSNBC anchor announcing that there had been a shooting in a Black church. With only 140 characters to spare, the tweet was short and declarative, yet my heart sank. The chances that it wasn't racially motivated seemed nil. I turned on the TV and watched the news for as long as I could stomach. My heart grew heavy as my eyes took it in. My beloved Church had been attacked again.

I've never stepped foot in Mother Emanuel, the loving nickname for that Charleston church. I don't know any of the congregation members, and I had never heard the name of its beloved pastor, or of any of the people killed that night. And yet, despite the geographical gap, it felt as if my own home church had been violated. The goal of terror attacks, after all, is to inspire fearfulness beyond the target.

It worked.

Until June 17, 2015, I had never been afraid of walking into a Black church. Black churches are gracious and hospitable, loving and welcoming, filled with people who like hugs and can't wait for the opportunity to speak goodness into your life. Even the shooter, on the very night of the rampage, had been a recipient of this love. And while many Black churches have members and pastors who are politically active, I had never carried the fear of church bombings or that local heroes would be victims of political assassinations—these were fears my parents, my grandparents, and my great-grandparents had known. That was all past, or so I thought, until the terror gripped my heart.

My fear lasted through the night, while the shooter remained at large. What if he went to another church? Would there be more death that night? Was the shooter working alone, or had a group of white terrorists spread out across the city—or, God forbid, the country? When I fell asleep that night, I still didn't know. And even when I woke up the next morning and discovered he'd been captured, the fear remained. What if the shooting inspired copycats? I deeply resented that the next time I walked into my own church, I would be afraid to sit with my back to the door.

That resentment turned into anger, and anger into defiance. I got up, got dressed, drove to a quiet church, and cried.

I cried for the lost lives of Cynthia Graham Hurd, Susie Jackson, Ethel Lance, Depayne Middleton-Doctor, Clementa Pinckney, Tywanza Sanders, Daniel Simmons, Sharonda Coleman-Singleton, and Myra Thompson. I cried for the family members and friends who would miss them.

I cried for the survivors who watched people they love die in front of them. I cried for the congregation members who would never be the same.

But I also cried for me. I cried not because I felt sorry for myself but because—in spite of all I had witnessed in the previous year—I still wanted to believe that America had become better than this. *Ain't no friends here,* I heard Dr. Simms's voice in my head, and the tears could not be stopped. I had wanted to believe that some things were now off-limits. But I was wrong. I underestimated the enduring power, the lethal imagination, the insatiable desire for blood of white supremacy. And I felt stupid. I should've known better. Had I not spent the last year writing about the persistence and deadliness of hatred for the Black body? It hurt to know America could still hurt me.

For all their talk about being persecuted, white Christian Americans don't know this kind of terror. Generations of Black Americans have known nothing but this kind of terror.

Allowing the reality of the moment to settle around me, that the past is still present, that racial hatred can still take our bodies in mass, I had to return to Black writers who understood the pain of societal hatred. Ntozake Shange wrote the following in her exquisite choreopoem, *For Colored Girls*

Who Have Considered Suicide When the Rainbow Is Enuf:

> *i thot i waz but i waz so stupid i waz able to be*
>   *hurt*
> *& that's not real*
> *not anymore*
> *i shd be immune*

In this particular poem, Shange writes in the voice of a woman who can't believe love has crushed her once again. But for me, this poem puts words to my relationship with America. I know the surreal feeling of believing I have achieved immunity from racial hatred only to feel the sting once again. I ought to be immune by now; I know too much about our racial history to be surprised. I've learned about slavery and lynchings, about white riots and bombings. It's not fair that my knowledge doesn't save me, that I can still be hurt. But I am human. I am human. And I am still alive.

Even when the world doesn't believe that Black bodies are capable of love. Even when it doesn't believe that I survive on intimacy, that I need other beings for love. Even when I would prefer to be immune, I am human. I demand intimacy. I demand tomorrow. I demand love.

As I cried and prayed and sang in an empty church sanctuary that afternoon, I knew what I needed to do next. For the first time in years, I needed to return to my childhood church with the green carpet and giant double doors. I needed to be with my daddy. I needed to go back, and that Sunday I did.

Turned out the carpet was no longer green—but all the important things were still the same. We still held hands while praying at the altar. Pastor still wiped his forehead with the same white towels after preaching. Church mothers still sat on the front row, and ushers still passed out fans with MLK on one side and a funeral home advertisement on the other. The choir still sang.

How excellent! How excellent! How excellent!
iiiiiiis your naaaaame!
Jesus, is the sweetest name I knoooooow.
My soul is anchored. My soul is anchored. My my
my my soul is anchored in the Lord.

Our voices grew stronger with each song. We would not let our generations of worship be halted by terror. Like so many times before, we found safety in one another and discovered that the Spirit delighted in who we are: in our praise, in our proclamation, in our prayers—but also in our person. The Spirit moved through our brown hands lifted in surrender, our hips swaying to the organ, our rich voices lifted in song. The Spirit moved among us. The Spirit was with us, just as she had always been. We would go on.

That Sunday also happened to be Children's Sunday, when the kids of the church prepared Scripture readings to deliver before the congregation. There was not a dry eye in the place as those little brown faces recited words of hope—some with bold confidence and others shyly repeating the words of the children's pastor. It didn't matter. They were here. We were here. We would go on. God would be with us.

I cried all the way through that service and many times in the days that followed. America had reawakened me to the power of its devastation. I recognized that history is still on repeat. Four little girls in 1963. Nine Black parishioners in 2015. But I also experienced again the love of other beings. I was surviving on the intimacy of the Black community—online, in real life, in the Church and outside of it. I was baptized again into the tradition of Black love—love for self and love for one another when the world deems us unworthy of life itself. We would stand and declare that our lives mattered. And as the days went on, and we kept protesting, organizing, marching, writing, and creating, I knew I could face tomorrow.

Interlude:

A Letter to My Son

My sweet son,

Even as I type this, you are tumbling around in my belly. You are only two pounds in weight, so your kicks feel like flutters, like butterflies in my stomach. You are my butterfly.

I often wonder if you will be as active as you feel. Will you play basketball or join the swim team? Will you climb trees and jump in puddles? Will you beg your daddy to learn karate and scare me to death by jumping off tables and couches and shopping carts and playground bars? Or will you prefer to stay inside? Will you forever have your head in a book? Will you be like your uncle and have an obsession with computers? Or will you be more like your aunts, with a flair for the artistic? I wonder about your developing personality. I wonder what the church mothers will prophetically declare about your future.

Your daddy and I talk about you all the time. He can't wait to show you all his favorite films, and he hopes you will like horror movies as much as he does. I think about taking you to the park, and indulging in my own childish sense of curiosity at the world, seeing it through your eyes anew. We wonder about the shape of your eyes, the sound of your laugh, the feel of your toes. We wonder how much you will cry. Your daddy is already dreaming of the day when you will join him in the barbershop for your first taper.

And though you are still being formed in my tummy, your father and I are slowly turning into parents—wondering more about your future than about our own. While we delight in these conversations about who and what you will become in life, we have been avoiding other conversations.

We have avoided talking about the first time some-one will call you a nigger. We have been avoiding talk-ing about the first time you will be pulled over by a cop because you look suspicious. We have been avoiding talking about the many assumptions people will have of you simply because God kissed your glorious skin and it blushed at the attention. We have avoided discussing how we will tell you about the world.

Of course we will. But we don't like to think of it yet. We would rather wonder if you will be precocious or subdued, bold or shy, funny or serious, adventurous or introspective. We would rather wonder about your humanity than ruminate on the ways the world will try to take that away from you. They will first think you are beautiful, innocent—and you will be. But as your baby fat disappears and your height comes to match ours, they will start to see you as dangerous—but we will be here to refute the lies. We will be here to remind you that you are worthy of joy and love and adventure.

In our house, there will be dancing. There will be laughter. There will be love. In our house, there will be the smell of soul food and the sound of Stevie. We will teach you all of Michael Jackson's moves, and we will let you stay up late to watch the NBA finals with your dad. There will also be tears. It won't be all joy all the time, and yet you, too, will be inducted into this blessing called Black love. It will undergird you and push you. It will envelop you and warm you. It will remind you of who you are. And we will be the first to welcome you into this divine community of hope.

For now, you keep tumbling around and around in my tummy. (Maybe consider taking a break at night.) I will never be able to protect you as I can now. So, you stay safe and grow strong. Though we are crazy scared, stupidly excited—we can't wait to meet you when the time comes.

Love,

Your Momma

13

Justice, Then Reconciliation

Racial reconciliation has become something of a buzzword in Christian circles. Churches refer to themselves as "multicultural" and uplift their missions work as evidence that they are making a difference in the world. But though the term has powerful implications for how Christians should pursue racial justice and multiracial community, you could be forgiven for thinking *reconciliation* is just a churchy-sounding catchall for any kind of diversity effort.

It's worth being clear; *reconciliation* is not a fancy word for any of the following:

- There are lots of [insert ethnicity here] people in my church.

- A multiethnic church
- Sharing a building with another, more diverse congregation
- Having one or two people of color and/or women on your leadership team
- Diversity that's represented only in custodial positions
- Asking lots of racial questions over a cup of coffee
- Celebrating various ethnicities and cultures every month
- Missions work
- Outreach work
- Urban ministry

Too often, attempts at reconciliation go no further than the items on this list—and when this happens, the word becomes commonplace, drained of its extraordinary power. In its true form, reconciliation possesses the impossible power of the lion lying down with the lamb; the transformative power of turning swords into plowshares. But instead of pushing for relationships that are deep, transformative, and just—instead of allowing these efforts to alter our worldview, deepen our sense of connectedness, and inspire us toward a generosity that seeks to make all things right—we have allowed *reconciliation* to become synonymous with *contentedly hanging out together.*

Reconciliation is not a magic word that we can trot out whenever we need healing or inspiration. Deep down, I think we know this is true, because our efforts to partake of an easy reconciliation have proved fruitless in the world. Too often, our discussions of race are emotional but not strategic, our outreach work remains paternalistic, and our ethnic celebrations fetishize people of color. Many champions of racial justice in the Church have stopped using the term altogether, because it has been so watered down from its original potency.

In their book *Radical Reconciliation,* Curtiss DeYoung and Allan Boesak unpack why this happens. They write, "reconciliation is revolutionary, that is, oriented to structural change." Which means, reconciliation can never be apolitical. Reconciliation chooses sides, and the side is always justice.

This is why white American churches remain so far from experiencing anything resembling reconciliation. The white Church considers power its birthright rather than its curse. And so, rather than seeking reconciliation, they stage moments of racial harmony that don't challenge the status quo. They organize worship services where the choirs of two racially different churches sing together, where a pastor of a different race preaches a couple times a year, where they celebrate MLK but don't acknowledge current racial injustices. Acts like these can create beautiful moments of harmony and goodwill, but since they don't change the underlying power structure at the organization, it would be misleading to call them acts of reconciliation. Even worse, when they're not paired with greater change, diversity efforts can have the opposite of their intended effect. They keep the church feeling good, innocent, maybe even progressive, all the while preserving the roots of injustice.

When an organization confuses diversity or inclusion with reconciliation, it often shows up in an obsession with numbers. How many Black people are in the photo? Has the 20 percent quota been met, so that we can call ourselves multicultural? Does our publication have enough stories written by people of color? Are there enough people of color on the TV show? But without people of color in key positions, influencing topics of conversation, content, direction, and vision, whatever diversity is included is still essentially white—it just adds people of color like sprinkles on top. The cake is still vanilla.

When this happens, people of color in the organization get saddled with the task of constantly fixing the harm done by halfhearted diversity efforts. We find ourselves challenging hiring decisions that don't reflect the company's stated commitment to diversity, pushing allies to speak up in rooms where marginalized voices aren't represented, responding to events or sermons that didn't go far enough (or worse, sermons that perpetuated harmful ideas). But must we always be the prophetic voice, the dissenter, the corrector, the fixer? Organizations would be wise to tap Black women in helping to craft the direction of the organization, the vision of the publication, the purpose of the ministry. When our voices are truly desired, numbers will cease to be the sole mark of achievement.

Here's another misconception. A great many people believe that reconciliation boils down to dialogue: a conference on race, a lecture, a moving sermon about the diversity we'll see in heaven. But dialogue is productive toward reconciliation only when it leads to action—when it inverts power and pursues justice for those who are most marginalized. Unfortunately, most "reconciliation conversations" spend most of their time teaching white people about racism. In too many churches and organizations, listening to the hurt and pain of people of color is the end of the road, rather than the beginning.

I am convinced that one of the reasons white churches favor dialogue is that the parameters of dialogue can be easily manipulated to benefit whiteness. Tone policing takes priority over listening to the pain inflicted on people of color. People of color are told they should be nicer, kinder, more gracious, less angry in their delivery, or that white people's needs, feelings, and thoughts should be given equal weight. But we cannot negotiate our way to reconciliation. White people need to listen, to pause so that people of color can clearly articulate both the disappointment they've endured and what it would take for reparations to be made. Too often, dialogue functions as a stall tactic, allowing white people to believe they've done something heroic when the real work is yet to come.

Fortunately, dialogue isn't the only way to participate in the creative work of justice and reconciliation. In fact, I suspect that other actions—marches and protests, books and Scripture, art and sermons, and active participation in coalitions seeking change— are equally transformative. But when white organizations rest on their laurels and demand that people of color only express gratefulness for past change, these creative efforts stall. They tell us we should be happy to be onstage, singing or playing those drums. We should be happy to have our staff position, or happy that they *gave us the chance* to write that book, lead that program, teach that class, or speak at that conference at all. And when we suggest that justice might require greater representation in leadership, greater access to funding, greater influence over mission or strategy, people of color find themselves hitting a wall. *Ain't no friends here.*

When white people stop short of reconciliation, it's often because they are motivated by a deep need to believe in their own goodness, and for that goodness to be affirmed over and over and over again. These folks want a pat on the back simply for arriving at the conclusion that having people of color around is good. But reconciliation is not about white feelings. It's about diverting power and attention to the oppressed, toward the powerless. It's not enough to dabble at diversity and inclusion while leaving the existing authority structure in place. Reconciliation demands more.

Reconciliation is the pursuit of the impossible—an upside-down world where those who are powerful have relinquished that power to the margins. It's reimagining an entirely different way of being with one another. Reconciliation requires imagination. It requires looking beyond what is to what could be. It looks beyond intentions to real outcomes, real hurts, real histories. How just, how equitable can our efforts be? What would it take to enact reparations, to make all things right?

Reconciliation is what Jesus does. When sin and brokenness and evil tore us from God, it was Jesus who reconciled us, whose body imagined a different relationship, who took upon himself the cross and became peace.

> Therefore, if anyone is in Christ, he is a new creation. The old has passed away; behold, the new has come. All this is from God, who through Christ reconciled us to himself and gave us the ministry of reconciliation; that is, in Christ God was reconciling the world to himself, not counting their trespasses against them, and entrusting to us the message of reconciliation.
>
> 2 CORINTHIANS 5:17–19

Reconciliation is ministry that belongs to Jesus. Jesus, who left the comfort of heaven and put on flesh, experiencing the beauty and brutality of being human. Jesus, who died on a cross and rose from the grave, making a way for all humanity to be joined in union with God. Through this divine experience of death, life, and reunion, we find the capacity for the work. In this, we see why reconciliation can transform not just our hearts or our churches but one day the whole world.

Fortunately, Jesus doesn't need all white people to get onboard before justice and reconciliation can be achieved. For me, this is freedom. Freedom to tell the truth. Freedom to create. Freedom to teach and write without burdening myself with the expectation that I can change anyone. It has also shifted my focus. Rather than making white people's reactions the linchpin that holds racial justice together, I am free to link arms with those who are already being transformed. Because at no point in America's history did all white people come together to correct racial injustice. At no point did all white people decide chattel slavery should end. At no point did all white people decide we should listen to the freedom fighters, end segregation, and enact the right of Black Americans to vote. At no point have all white people gotten together and agreed to the equitable treatment of Black people. And yet there has been change, over time, over generations, over history.

The march toward change has been grueling, but it is real. And all it has ever taken was the transformed—the people of color confronting past and present to imagine a new future, and the handful of white people willing to release indifference and join the struggle.

14

Standing in the Shadow of Hope

Christians talk about love a lot. It's one of our favorite words, especially when the topic is race.

> If we could just learn to love one another . . .
> Love trumps hate . . .
> Love someone different from you today . . .

But I have found this love to be largely inconsequential. More often than not, my experience has been that whiteness sees love as a prize it is owed, rather than a moral obligation it must demonstrate. Love, for whiteness, dissolves into a demand for grace, for niceness, for endless patience—to keep everyone feeling comfortable while hearts are being changed. In this way, so-called love dodges any responsibility for action and waits for the great catalytic moment that finally spurs accountability.

I am not interested in love that is aloof. In a love that refuses hard work, instead demanding a bite-size education that doesn't transform anything. In a love that qualifies the statement "Black lives matter," because it is unconvinced this is true. I am not interested in a love that refuses to see systems and structures of injustice, preferring to ask itself only about personal intentions.

This aloof kind of love is useless to me.

I need a love that is troubled by injustice. A love that is provoked to anger when Black folks, including our children, lie dead in the streets. A love that can no longer be concerned with tone because it is concerned with life. A love that has no tolerance for hate, no excuses for racist decisions, no contentment in the status quo. I need a love that is fierce in its resilience and sacrifice. I need a love that chooses justice.

But I have learned that when I expect this kind of love for my Black female body, it means inviting hopelessness to my doorstep.

Hopelessness and I have become good friends.

When Ta-Nehisi Coates released his landmark book *Between the World and Me,* a stunning memoir of Black life in America, much of the talk in both secular and Christian circles revolved around the question of hope. Was Coates being too cynical by describing race relations to his son in such bleak terms? Why write such a depressing book? Is Coates that hopeless in real life? People read his words about America—about its history, about its present, about the realities of living in a Black body—and then demanded hopefulness. It boggles the mind.

For me, Coates's words contain relief in that they were spoken aloud, in public, with the forcefulness history demands. But talking about race in America is not usually a hopeful experience if you're Black. It brings no pleasure to speak of the hatred inflicted on our souls, the stories of discrimination and pain and injustices large and small that populate our lives. At the same time, we are barraged by society's reinforcement that we are less than. I may be grieving the murder of Trayvon Martin and at the same time dodging the inquisitive fingers of a white woman reaching to touch my hair. I may be angry over the events in Ferguson and in the same moment attempting to respond with dignity to a white man who treats me as his verbal punching bag. I may have just heard about the latest racist words spewed by a white talk-show host, actor, or politician on the same day when I'm trying to claim my space in the classroom or on my college campus. The persistence of racism in America—individual and societal—is altogether overwhelming. It doesn't lay the best fertilizer for hope to grow.

And so hope for me has died one thousand deaths. I hoped that friend would get it, but hope died. I hoped that person would be an ally for life, but hope died. I hoped that my organization really desired change, but hope died. I hoped I'd be treated with the full respect I deserve at my job, but hope died. I hoped that racist policies would change, and just policies would never be reversed, but hope died. I hoped the perpetrator in uniform would be brought to justice this time, but hope died. I hoped history would stop repeating itself, but hope died. I hoped things would be better for my children, but hope died.

So I have learned not to fear the death of hope. In order for me to stay in this work, hope must die. I do not enjoy the tears that come from these great disappointments. I do not look forward to future racialized traumas. I don't really want to recount all the ways that hope has let me down; it's so damn painful. But all of this comes with living, with struggling, with believing in the possibility of change. The death of hope gives way to a sadness that heals, to anger that inspires, to a wisdom that empowers me the next time I get to work, pick up my pen, join a march, tell my story.

The death of hope begins in fury, ferocious as a wildfire. It feels uncontrollable, disastrous at first, as if it will destroy everything in the vicinity—but in the midst of the fury, I am forced to find my center. What is left when hope is gone? What is left when the source of my hope has failed? Each death of hope has been painful and costly. But in the mourning there always rises a new clarity about the world, about the Church, about myself, about God.

And in this there is new life. Realignment. Rediscovery.

And on the really good days: renewal.

I cannot hope in whiteness. I cannot hope in white people or white institutions or white America. I cannot hope in lawmakers or politicians, and I cannot hope even in pastors or ministries or mission statements. I cannot hope in misquoted wisdom from MLK, superficial ethnic heritage celebrations, or love that is aloof. I cannot hope even in myself. I am no one's savior. The longer this list gets, the more elusive hope becomes.

And so, instead of waiting for the bright sunshine, I have learned to rest in the shadow of hope.

Shortly after the publication of his book, Ta-Nehisi Coates was asked if he had reason to hope that racism in America will one day change. He responded:

> Slavery in this country was 250 years. What that means is that there were African Americans who were born in this country in 1750/1760 and if they looked backwards their parents were slaves. Their grandparents were slaves. Their great grandparents were slaves. If they looked forward, their children would be slaves. Their grandchildren would be slaves. And possibly, their great grandchildren will be slaves. There was no real hope within their individual life span of ending enslavement—the most brutal form of degradation in this country's history. There was nothing in their life that said, "This will end in my lifetime. I will see the end of this." And they struggled. And they resisted.

This is the shadow of hope. Knowing that we may never see the realization of our dreams, and yet still showing up. I do not believe that I or my children or my grandchildren will live in an America that has achieved racial equality. I do not believe this is a problem that America will fix within any soon-coming generation. And so I stand in the legacy of all that Black Americans have already accomplished—in their resistance, in their teachings, in their voices, in their faith—and I work toward a world unseen, currently unimaginable. I am not enslaved, and yet I look back and see centuries of creative evolution of the hatred for Black bodies. I look at the present—police brutality, racial disparities, backlash against being "politically correct," hatred for our first Black president, the gutting of the Voting Rights Act, and the election of a chief executive who stoked the fire of racial animosity to win—and I ask myself, *Where is your hope, Austin?* The answer: It is but a shadow.

It is working in the dark, not knowing if anything I do will ever make a difference. It is speaking anyway, writing anyway, loving anyway. It is enduring disappointment and then getting back to work. It is knowing this book may be read only by my Momma, and writing it anyway. It is pushing back, even though my words will never be big enough, powerful enough, weighty enough to change everything. It is knowing that God is God and I am not.

This is the cool place from where I demand a

love that matters. In this place, I see the sun setting behind me, its light as far away as the stars, and I let the limitations of hope settle over me. I possess not the strength of hope but its weakness, its fragility, its ability to die. Because I must demand anyway. It is my birthright. It is the culmination of everything my ancestors endured, of all that my parents taught me, of the Blackness that rescued me. How dare I consider surrender simply because I want the warmth of the sun? This warmth has not been promised to me. My faith does not require it.

When the sun happens to shine, I bask in the rays. But I know I cannot stay there. That is not my place to stand. So I abide in the shadows, and let hope have its day and its death. It is my duty to live anyway.

ACKNOWLEDGMENTS

There are so many people who have supported me on this journey in so many ways; I am not sure how to make these words convey the amount of gratitude I feel.

First, I want to thank everyone who literally made this book possible. Thank you to my agent, Rachelle Gardner, for all the phone calls, meetings, and notes (and for making me practice saying "I am a writer" until I believed it). Thanks also to Derek Reed, my editor, for putting up with my firm belief that grammar only exists to make the sentences sound the way I would want them read aloud. Thanks to Convergent for taking a chance on this new author and giving yourselves to this book. To David Kopp, Tina Constable, Campbell

Wharton, Carisa Hays, Megan Schumann, Nick Stewart, Ayelet Gruenspecht, Ashley Hong, Jessie Bright, Norman Watkins, Ada Yonenaka, and Songhee Kim, my deepest gratitude for your time, energy, and creative brilliance.

Next I must thank the family members and friends who lent me their memories when mine failed. I am so honored to be able to call, text, DM, email and tweet you without ever wondering if I will hear back from you. Your responses to my questions, the sharing of memories, made this a less lonely writing project.

To my early readers, you made this book better. Thank you for your honest feedback, critique, questions, and suggestions.

There are a host of mentors who introduced me to the publishing world, supported my writing early on, and regularly encouraged me throughout this process. I could not have done this without you all.

Thank you to my parents whose excitement has never waned over the long life of this project. Thank you for your support, from teaching me the ABCs to listening to me when I am all out of words.

Lastly, I must thank my wonderful husband, Tommie Brown. Years ago, with tears in my eyes and the blanket pulled over my head, I asked you if writing was just the dream of a teenage girl—a dream I needed to let go. I fully expected you to tell me it was time to grow up and stop trying. But you held my hand, wiped away the tears, and believed in me when I was too scared to hope anymore. Thank you for taking such good care of my heart, that day and every day since. I love you.